Letters From Your Inner Being

Trista Ainsworth

Published by Trista Ainsworth, 2024.

While every precaution has been taken in the preparation of this book, the publisher assumes no responsibility for errors or omissions, or for damages resulting from the use of the information contained herein.

LETTERS FROM YOUR INNER BEING

First edition. November 11, 2024.

Copyright © 2024 Trista Ainsworth.

ISBN: 979-8227795083

Written by Trista Ainsworth.

Table of Contents

Foreward by Melissa Bee 1
Introduction 4
An exercise you can try is this: 79
Make a list of the following loose ends you may need to take care of: 99
Here is a list of things to consider: 158
Notes of Gratitude for Letters From Your Inner Being 167
About the author 169
About Melissa Bee 170

For my favorite human beings: Paul and Adam

Foreword by Melissa Bee

Sharing my passion for this powerful book, written by one of my dearest friends, Trista Ainsworth, is an absolute blessing.

Not too long ago, Trista shared a memory we had 4 years ago, when her heart spoke up for the messages she was receiving from The Universe. When she felt compelled to write this book.

The memory reminded Trista and I of the long road that has led here- of the complete and utter belief I have in her. I knew then that, one day, she would make her dreams a reality while simultaneously inspiring others with the powerful messages that are within each of us.

So, yes, my love for this book began 4 years ago when I knew its greatness was being born, but intensely magnified when I read it. The words encapsulated me in instanteous love.

I knew she would create wonder, but could not imagine the impact it would have on me until it was in my hands.

The timing was impeccable.

During the time Trista introduced me to this precious creation, I was finishing my degree, interning, and taking care of my three children. Life was hectic and times were difficult, but I remember reading:

"The words on these pages will help you grow in any situation."

At that moment, the book spoke to me loud and clear. The overwhelming situation I was in beckoned me to intensify the positive voices within me to propel me to a higher level of growth.

The messages in Trista's book helped me grow with love, encouragement, understanding and guidance.

This book is like having the bestest friend in the world with you, showering you with love and kindness when you need it the most.

The words in this book continue to make a powerful impact on my life and I know it will do the same for yours.

It's funny how the universe works. Writing connected me to Trista, and now Trista is connecting me back to writing. I am beyond grateful for all of these connections, especially the human ones, like the one I have with Trista.

Thank you for your connection that began as soon as you opened this book.

Congratulations on embarking on this journey, reading the loving messages your inner light joyously wants to share with you.

On purpose, this book is in your hands. On purpose, the time has come for you to read it.

These letters are purposely uplifting reminders designed to shift the negativity you may endure.

The universe is purposely reaching out to you, lifting you up, and is about to securely and lovingly carry you away.

It is no secret that as we continue down the path of life, thunderous noise echoes through our souls. However, as the obstacles we face as sure as the sun shines, we still fight to overcome our individual and collective struggle.

We feel great pain and can be consumed by the chaos surrounding us.

Yes, the sound of the negative messages are loud!

It is difficult, many times impossible, to listen to the light of our inner voices.

However, now we have our inner voice in the open as we see the words illuminated right in front of us.

What a blessing!

I hope you seek the bright light in your hands, when the world and your thoughts wear you down, may you reach for these letters and turn the darkness off.

Melissa

Introduction

Dear Human Being,
It is no accident you came upon these letters! Our message to you is one of eternal hope and light. Our Earth and all human beings need these words today. The following letters bring you love from our hearts to yours. Know that we accompany you every day to push you forward. The words on these pages will help you grow in any situation.

You are someone with talents and gifts to give everyone.

We implore you to use your gifts to uplift others every day. Do not let your gifts and love wither and die without coming into the light for all to enjoy. The time is now!

Everyone has a big dream buried within their heart. It is the moment to start unearthing it, treating it with loving care, and taking action to bring it to life.

Even if you only feel a small glimmer of joy emerging, use that spark to propel you in the right direction. You know deep in your heart what you need to do. Dreaming is a beautiful way to activate your emotions and add fuel to the fire of your desires in life.

Once your thoughts solidify, write down your dreams and goals. Those are the keys to sharing your gifts with the world.

We look forward to assisting you in every way possible! Find inspiration, solace, peace, and love within these pages when you need a boost in life. We love you more than you can possibly know.

With the greatest love ever,
Your Inner Being

Note: Sometimes your Inner Being refers to itself as I and sometimes as we. It may be a single voice or a collective voice.

Dear Human Being,

I know some days can be confusing for you. Others around you may be angry, upset, or not loving.

Please know that they feel pain.

They are not angry with you. Sometimes, those around you do not know how to diffuse the pain. I know it hurts your sensitive heart.

Know that they love you in their own way. They may not know how to express their love because they feel too much anguish. It is as if their hearts are too full of despair.

Even when others break your heart, I am here for you.

I am here to help you shine the light inside you for all to see. You were born upon this Earth for a specific reason.

The confusion, pain, and hurt you sometimes feel through experiences with others are designed to grow the compassion in your heart. As it grows, you can understand and relate to them.

We all came here to learn the most valuable lessons in the universe.

This mission is not always easy to complete, but that is why you are here. You are the one to decode and comprehend the most difficult parts of life.

I believe in you!

Your heart speaks, and I listen.

Sending you infinite love today,

Your Inner Being

Dear Human Being,

I understand you are overwhelmed by the emotions of others. There are times in life when clouds come to cover your loving heart.

Fear not, as I am here to soothe the pain when it comes.

My love is steadfast and always here for you to lean on when others cascade their emotions upon you. I know you are strong, but sometimes you need some time to regain strength.

I am here to make sure you still have light inside you to move forward. Hold on and know I am here for you.

I never waver from your heart center, no matter what happens. I help to soothe those inner wounds that take a toll on your spirit.

You have an enormous capacity for love. It is why some words linger in the air and hurt you for days afterward. However, you will be able to take one step forward every day.

The bright light inside you will never extinguish. It will only be illuminated more with each passing day.

I hold infinite love for you,

Your Inner Being

Dear Human Being,

I love it when you wake up on a fresh morning full of hope and possibility. I feel your deep connection with the source of all beings on days like this. I know you experience it, too.

On a day when you start out with joy, you can create anything.

I want you to know that no matter what, I am here holding that pure light for you.

I am here on days like this one and darker ones. I am the one to hold space for you so that you may shine bright when you are ready.

Today, you have prepared your heart to do great work.

You will spread the bright light with your smile and the message you have to share. It is something I love to witness.

It is my purpose within you. I want to hold you steady in admiration, knowing that you will unlock your full potential on days when you are ready.

I hold no judgment for you on days that are not as joyful, but I know you will return to your light after the storms of life subside.

Today, go forth and create as it is why you were born, just at the right time for humanity to benefit from your positive spirit.

With infinite love,
Your Inner Being

Dear Human Being,

On days like today, I notice the spark in your heart. You are starting to believe in yourself and the enormous gift you have to give the world.

Never doubt that you are here to do something only you can do. You decided long before you were born into this life what your mission would be.

I know that vision can be clouded by the difficulties of life. However, I am always here, understanding the potential of your spirit.

As you take on the day with a positive spirit, you begin to fulfill your destiny.

Never doubt that your light is always with you.

I never waver on your path, even when you do. I stand steady, ready to catch you if you start to fall. It is natural to stumble at times, weighed down by burdens.

When you decide to reach down for the strength of your light, that is me smiling at you.

Today is a day I see your light in full force, and you are ready to share with everyone.

If I could show up in form, I would be cheering and holding a sign that says: Go for it!

Please know that I am your internal cheerleader!

Love,

Your Inner Being

Dear Human Being,

I know some days you wake up with doubt in your mind. It can be hard to set out on your daily path without reassurance.

The road to your destiny is paved with hope.

The seeds of doubt are sometimes planted, but your heart is strong. I am here to give you strength in the moments you feel weak.

Lean on me and know that you are held in my love.

Your mission here may not always be clear, but if you reach into your heart, you will find the map to where you need to go.

My love and confidence in you are always here to steady you even when you falter.

Doubt is sometimes planted within you, but you can prevent it from clouding your vision of a better world.

I know you want the best for humanity, the universe, and everyone you hold dear. That is why you are here, to do something you chose long ago.

Each day, I provide a glimmer of what your mission is. You can go forth and deliver it to the world.

I believe in you always,
Your Inner Being

Dear Human Being,

We know you are reaching out of your comfort zone toward a big goal. It can feel dangerous at times. However, we want you to know we are behind you.

Deciding to be a part of the world is a beautiful way to shine your light.

Do not hide in the shadows. You will not allow your life's mission to come out to the forefront.

You are here to do something nobody else can.

That may be challenging to understand sometimes. However, we know that once you take one step on the path, you can take one more step each day.

Give yourself time, grace, and love along the way.

We are here to hold your heart steady. There is nothing you cannot handle because we are always here to catch you if you fall on a stone.

Yes, there will be obstacles, disappointments, and setbacks.

Those are there for you to teach you to gain strength, courage, and love along the way. Without those teachings, you would not be as strong, bright, and capable as you are.

Even when days are dark, we hold the lantern of your spirit so that you can continue on your path.

We love you always,

Your Inner Being

Dear Human Being,

Your determination to reach your goals is outstanding!

We have been observing you lately. We know you are about to achieve amazing feats. The effort you put in every day will have a cumulative effect on your life. It may seem to only be a simple routine, but your work will multiply for you.

We are so proud of you for the resolve you show.

Some days, you may be more motivated to work on your goals than others. It is paramount to follow through even if the motivation is not there.

Sit with your creativity, hoping, wishing, and praying for an outcome. Please know it is always coming to you. You may not see it now, but your dreams are swirling and ready to meet you.

When you do your work diligently, you show us you are ready.

You are ready to receive the goodness of the universe for the giving person that you are. You give from your heart when you create something to go out into the world.

You are going through many trials in life, and sometimes, it may seem like your work does not matter. Know that you are creating the foundation for a miracle. However small your daily contribution is, it is part of a plan for everyone.

We cannot wait to see your work come to fruition. We know sometimes it is hard to be content with the small breadcrumbs in your existence. We promise you will understand why you must carry out your work with love.

You carry the light of love in your heart, and we love you daily.

Keep on shining your light,

Your Inner Being

Dear Human Being,

We love it when you have a burst of joyful energy come into your life. It is like a beam of light coming from your heart.

It lights up everything around you, causing you to feel happiness and peace.

That feeling helps you continue on your path. We are here to ignite those sparks of encouragement. Feel everything around you, as it contains energy to keep you going.

Sometimes, you smile, laugh, and sing.

We love to see this happen, as it is a sign of knowing we are here to help you keep that joy within you at all times. When it bubbles up to the surface, you feel happy and connected to the world.

It can occur at any time, even during the most ordinary moments.

The longer you stay in this energy field, the more you can create. You will encounter more courage within you to keep going.

It is as if your heart were an energy generator. As you heal emotionally, you can feel more joy. Your energy rises. It is so beautiful to witness this. When it happens, we celebrate with you.

What a joy to see you fly on a carpet of happiness.

We know how it makes you feel. It is the best feeling in the world!

We love you infinitely,

Your Inner Being.

Dear Human Being,

It lights me up when you find happiness in your heart.

I am always here, cheering you on. However, I find more energy to send your way when you choose happiness and joy.

Some days, it is easier to choose these emotions than others.

I understand that there cannot be light without darkness sometimes.

Please know that I am always with you. I am here on the days you feel energy and light and days you feel darkness and despair.

I always live in a place of uplifting words.

In this way, I am ready to help you whenever you need me. I never waver from the light.

As a human being, I know you sometimes go off of your path. These are beautiful experiences because they teach you what you want in life.

What everyone always wants is joy.

I thank you for choosing joy when you can. You are a bright and shining light!

With love,

Your Inner Being.

Dear Human Being,

We love to see how much you value your dreams and goals. We hold their potential within us every day.

We see you when you rise early, hoping to put in extra time.

You are there making your dreams happen, and we hold the candle, cheering on your every move.

The light inside you burns bright. You can go down the path of your deepest desires. It is all there waiting for you to let it in.

The sparkles of your aims swirl around you, inviting you to participate in the celebration. When your energy is high, a smile of delight comes to your face. We smile in return, knowing you are taking action toward what will bring the most joy into your life.

These are the most beautiful moments in your life because you are being yourself. The joy in your heart comes into play in your creativity.

That is a beautiful thing to witness, and we have front-row seats.

Keep going towards that which you love. That is the path for you!

We love you at every moment, twist and turn in your path,

Your Inner Being.

Dear Human Being,

I wanted to let you know I see you every day, working hard towards your dreams. Some days, it may seem they are very far away from you. What I see is different.

Your dreams are all around you, circling you as you work towards them. They are sparkling stars right within your reach.

All you have to do is trust.

Trust in me, your inner being. I hold you in infinite love and wisdom at every moment of your life.

At times, it may seem the opposite. You keep working towards something, but it hasn't come yet. Let go and trust. I know it is a simple phrase, but it works.

Your destiny is right there within you.

I am there, holding your hand at every turn on your path. Your unique and creative talents touch hearts. That is why you are here. My job is to steady you, even when you want to stop.

Do not give up.

Your dreams are so close. I see them every day. At each moment, you are breathing, living, and experiencing life. You are living your dream.

I see you hoping, wishing, and praying.

I promise it is not in vain. We love you so much, and we will not let you fail.

With infinite love,
Your Inner Being

Dear Human Being,

We love your determination and positive energy. I know you can feel the support around you as you travel toward your destiny every day.

When you sit down to create your dreams, we are there.

We see, feel, and hear everything you do to bring your dream to fruition.

When you believe, we are there.

We hold doubt at bay for you as much as we can. We know you want to succeed and see everything you imagine in your life. They are waiting for you.

The more open, appreciative, and grateful you are, the more will flow to you.

Every day, you discover new ways to open up to the universe. We are holding the door open. You can go through that door daily or close it with negative thoughts.

The more you go towards the light, the more opportunities come.

We believe in your eternal power to create something beautiful for the world. You are here as a teacher, helping others to see their ultimate potential.

With love and understanding,
Your Inner Being

Dear Human Being,

I know some days doubt creeps into your thoughts. They are pervasive and do not allow your light to shine through.

In those days, you still have enormous power. You have to reach for it.

We are always here, showing you ways to recover your energy. We know that not all days can be high energy. There are things in your environment that cause you to doubt. However, we never doubt you.

Sometimes, all that is needed is to refocus.

A walk in nature, meditation, some grace, and peace always help to give you back your powerful energy to create and be one with the world.

You came here to spread your light to others. For that, you need high energy.

When it is low, it is paramount to take the time to replenish it. Do not worry about your work or to-do list. It will be here when your energy returns.

In the meantime, take a walk, light a candle, and sit in peace.

We love you always, at every moment,

Your Inner Being

Dear Human Being,

We love it when you wake up with determination and expect the best of yourself. On these days, you soar high!

From this elevated place, your dreams can begin to take shape.

We always visualize you up here, at this level. Even though sometimes you are not there, we hold you in this beautiful light.

Waking up from a high-flying place, knowing you can take on the world, gives you wings to fly. We always know you can make it there if you try.

Making a list of all your dreams and tasks you wish to accomplish is a loving step to take.

Once you speak or write the words, your wishes go into motion.

We see the wheels begin to turn, and destiny starts to follow. It is up to you to keep it going, but we know you will. You are never alone, looking for your dreams.

We are always here by your side, hoping and wishing for you! The universe always wants the best for you. You only need to allow your dreams to come true.

We appreciate your willingness to keep going, even on tough days.

We love you so much,

Your Inner Being

Dear Human Being,

We love to see you reach higher each day.

We know what you can do, and it is beyond your wildest dreams. We see it all the time.

It is such a beautiful sight to see you go for your dreams.

You can and will have everything you always dreamed of.

The path may not always be clear, and there will be mountains and valleys along the way. However, hold steady to your vision; beautiful things can happen.

Today, you have gathered so much momentum. You made a choice to go for something out of your comfort zone.

For this, we are so proud of you!

Love,

Your Inner Being

Dear Human Being,

We know you do not remember the agreement when you signed up for this life. You knew you came here to learn lessons and bring them back to us.

There was an awareness that you would have to go through a lot of darkness to find the light here on Earth.

It is the most challenging school.

We applaud you every day for your choice.

If you are reading this, it means you have a special mission to fulfill. You are a teacher, and you come here to spread love.

It is one of the most critical times on Earth. There is a call to focus on love, even through the ups and downs of life.

Each moment you choose to love everyone, your light grows.

This light and energy bring about change. At times, you may not see it.

Yet, it is there radiating a signal of hope to all humankind.

By enjoying each moment and living life to the fullest, you fulfill your destiny. We are thankful for your service.

With love and eternal light,

Your Soul Family

Dear Human Being,

We absolutely love it when you challenge yourself. We know what you are capable of.

You just needed to get up to speed with our belief in you.

We have always known your greatness and ability to connect with others. It is all right there in your heart. When you reach deep into your heart, you know you can do anything you set out to accomplish.

In this place where we reside, in your soul, we hold faith in you. There is never a doubt within us. We always know you can do what your heart desires. It is best to maintain a desire within you and let it flourish.

When you let your desires come out into the open, it is like stars getting to play and dance for the first time. It is pure delight!

The love we feel for you will never ever end.

Let the love you feel inside you carry you forward, past the obstacles that used to stand before you. You are stronger than you know.

With infinite love,
Your Inner Being

Dear Human Being,

When you start something challenging and new, you will wonder where the time went.

There is so much to learn, and you feel slow. The challenge of a new work adventure is paramount in your evolution as a human being.

If you do not try difficult things, you cannot grow.

We always applaud you for giving your best effort, come what may. It is such a beautiful thing to watch you try your best.

Please know that we always hold you in love and light, no matter what the day brings.

You can reach whatever goal you set for yourself. If you do not try, you cannot achieve what you came here to do.

By putting in a lot of effort, you grow.

As you struggle to learn a new skill, we are there smiling. We cheer your every move as you soldier on to become more of yourself. This gradual unfolding of all that you are is our ultimate triumph.

Keep doing what challenges you, and you will go far on your path. That is our sincere hope for you today and always.

Strive to be your best self.

In love and service,

Your Inner Being

Dear Human Being,

Does it feel that time flies by, and you do not know how you will accomplish everything on your list? Fear not.

We have the balance of time worked out for you. There will be enough moments in the day to do everything you wish. Slow down and savor the moments with those you love. This moment is precious, and in it is everything you desire.

Even when things seem to speed up, there is a universal balance.

When you breathe and relax into your day, you create more time. It does not seem possible, but it is. When you go for your dreams, time expands so you can do what is needed to reach your full potential.

We hold you in high esteem every day of your life. Every second that passes, we adore you. We love you when you are at rest and running at full speed.

When you find joy in what you do, that is the moment to rejoice. The flow of time will envelop you in a beautifully soft blanket, cradling you in a melody to help you finish your tasks. Time is ever abundant for those who live with joy.

We send you love at whatever moment you need it. It is like a little push from the universe to keep going towards that which makes you smile.

With love and gratitude,
Your Inner Being.

Dear Human Being,

When you are relaxed and being yourself, you are an exquisite being. You came here to experience everything and learn lessons.

Sometimes, those lessons can be painful and hurt your heart.

Yet, you have great beauty inside you. Beauty is a shining light that never goes dark. It illuminates you and your path even when you feel unsure.

When you trust us, we can guide you toward that which will fulfill your heart's desire. It is not a selfish way of being. It is the way of the universe.

Concentrate on what you do have and not what you lack, and you find peace. That calming force feels like freedom. The freedom to be who you are. Be you, and the world opens up to meet you with grace.

We know sometimes it is challenging to shine your light. You often want to hide. However, hiding your beauty robs the world of a gift.

Right now, we are all in need of healing. We seek to understand ourselves and break down the walls that separate our hearts. When everyone focuses on joy, we can make it.

Our inner knowing tells us you are the one.

You may think one being cannot solve everything, but just by coming here to learn, you are part of the solution. An elegant design is created for each situation you encounter so that you can find hope, love, and peace to share with others.

Sometimes, the pain is our teacher. Other times, it is love. We all learn at different paces.

You are here to create something unique for the Earth.

Thank you for being here with us,

Your Inner Being

Dear Human Being,

Today is your birthday!

It is the day you chose to make your first appearance on the Earth plane. You waited for this glorious moment with light in your eyes.

When you first emerged, you knew where you had come from in your soul family and your purpose here with everyone else. With each day that passed, you forgot a little more. That is by design.

At first, forgetting is paramount.

You learn lessons as they are here on this planet. It is the most challenging teacher you will ever know. Yet, you are one of the brave ones.

For this reason, you are reading these words. You now know you chose to experience everything to bring love and light to the world. We think the hard lessons are unfair and unjust, but they are there to guide you to your higher purpose.

Your birthday marks another year of growth and expansion. Your heart smiles.

We were here with you at that very first moment and will be with you until you go home to your spirit family. Some days, you may wish to be enveloped in the cocoon of your soul. However, know that your work here is not yet done.

Celebrate this day and all of this month with joy.

Every single second you are alive, we celebrate you. Yet, there is no ending to you. It is only the beginning. You are eternal, a living being who moves to another realm after this one is fulfilled. That brings peace to your heart.

We relish every smile that passes your lips. You are a bright soul.

We hold you in high esteem and endless love,

Your Inner Being

Dear Human Being,

Did you know we can see how much your heart and being sparkle and shine? They are brighter than the best-cut diamonds and crystals and more precious than the crown jewels.

When you choose to shine your light, you emanate an inner sparkle.

We are always waiting for you to choose this way of being. Those shimmers are remnants of your soul-being. It is how you looked with your soul family, translucent, shining, and full of light.

That is why you are called a light worker or light-being. It is because you shine from the inside out.

Sometimes, you do not feel full of light, but it always exists within you. All you have to do is feel joy and spread it to whoever you see on your path. They do not know they possess the same light.

Many have forgotten why they are here and feel downtrodden, in despair and sorrow. Your job is to lift them up with your light to the best of your ability.

That is why we seek to encourage you to stay strong. Your character and strength are needed right now. Someone is waiting for you to reach out and give a little sparkle of your light. It will help illuminate the way for them.

In turn, you receive light and goodness in your heart. It is how the world works. When we give with all our being, we see abundance for all of us.

Thank you for shining your sparkling light today. You are an example for all of us.

With love and gratitude,
Your Inner Being

Dear Human Being,

Sometimes, relationships with others can be challenging. They can even be confusing at times. You can love someone and need to let them find their own way.

We know it hurts your heart to not know what another person needs.

However, they will show you with their actions and their words. Allow them to be and do what is necessary for them to evolve. It may hurt and feel like they are no longer a part of your world, but they still love you in their own way.

Letting go means loving even more.

It seems like a contradiction, but it is not. It means loving from an even higher place because we are not attached to the outcome.

If someone declines your invitation many times but still reaches out from time to time, it means they still value their connection to you. They are still learning and figuring things out in life. They are walking their own path, which is needed for their growth.

Separation and space can help both of you to grow as light-filled beings. Each of you finds a different route, but we are all going home one day to our soul families with the lessons we learned along the way.

Keep reaching out to them. Tell them they are loved. Wait with eagerness but not disdain.

We promise you that they love everyone with all their heart. Each human being who came here to learn needs to receive lessons differently.

Love, forgiveness, and light help us learn to let go and trust all is well.

At every moment, the universe reaches out to us. It guides us as we help you with every step. Your loved one is the same. Do not be confused, dear one. Sometimes, silence is a teacher. Being quiet and going within allows us to become who we really are.

Perhaps the one you love is going within for the answers.

Take comfort in knowing you are right where you belong right now.
With eternal love,
Your Inner Being

Dear Human Being,

We love to see you doing your best every day. Some days, you may run short on time, but do not let that stop you from your dreams.

You chose to challenge yourself and grow.

Our guidance is always here to ensure you are on the right path. Do not fear. We will hold the balance for you.

Listen to the signs around you for the right time to take a break. When you stretch yourself, your dreams come true!

As the source of energy and light within you, you can grow. Be proud of what you are working on and trying to accomplish. It is a joy to see you soar!

Once in a while, you may take on too much at once.

It is because you are meant to stretch your wings and fly. You want to try your best to reach your goals and full potential. It is one of the most beautiful events here on Earth.

We witness heartache, pain, triumph, and joy. There are no limits, only growth points in life.

It is thrilling to feel you can go further than before.

Thank you for allowing us into your life.

With love and light,

Your Inner Being

Dear Human Being,

It is beautiful to feel fully prepared to start a new week. As you write your plans, we sense the joy in your heart. It flutters around like a butterfly seeking the nectar of a flower.

Making plans indicates you are going for your dreams.

Your spirit came here to understand what it was like to become a whole being. Having a calling to pursue each day is part of this mission.

When you even spend your free time doing what you love, that is a vocation of the highest order. We can tell when you are ready to give it your all. It is the best feeling in the world!

You will discover the more you do what you love, the more abundance will find you.

Stay committed to daily actions to take you further down the path of your dreams. We know you can step out into the unknown and feel lost.

Yet, we are always here with the light on, waiting for you to continue. Do not ever stop going for what you believe in. You can take time to rest, to breathe, to take the sights in, but do not give up.

Lay out your best plans, and we will help ensure they come to fruition.

Before you were born, the stars aligned. The universe conspires to put together everything you need to be a success. It is like creating a gift basket for all of humanity.

There is more than enough for everyone to choose from.

The more you believe in yourself, the more you can unfold what is there for you. Each action is a breadcrumb on your trail, leading you home to yourself.

If you could see how bright you shine as you once did with your soul family, you would never have a care in the world. You are a luminous being, and every part of you sparkles no matter what happens in the outside world.

We, your inner being, watch over everything in your life. Sometimes lessons come to you, but only when you are ready. That is why planning and dreaming are paramount for you. They bring your dreams to life.

Writing them on paper or saying them out loud is more magical. It sparks the universe to set about a chain reaction of perfect little miracles just for you.

You are the miracle we wait for each day. Each human being comes alive more at every moment. The awakening of the planet is happening because you choose to be you.

We love everything you do toward your deepest desires.

With infinite love,

Your Inner Being

LETTERS FROM YOUR INNER BEING

Dear Human Being,

You are now learning to use your intuition. That little nudge you feel to do something is deep in your inner knowing. We put it there, little by little.

Those fun little thoughts come up all of a sudden. That's us!

We love to have a good time here at your inner being HQ, always surprising you at every turn. If you stop to notice, we never stop showing you ways to feel joy.

The reason why we love to do this is simple. It makes you smile. Those little moments of joy are pure gold where we are from. We leave you little sparkles along your trail.

Notice when you feel called to do something. Pay attention when you cannot let go of a feeling. Those are clues to show you where you need to go.

It is even better if you get butterflies in your stomach. It causes you to feel and notice what is happening in your body and what it means. Every sign and signal is meaningful. Do not discount coincidences, repeated numbers, or rainbows.

Everything around you is meant to be there. We are here to remind you every day that you are exquisite.

If you start to forget, we put something in your path to remind you. A warm fuzzy feeling in your heart, the coziness of a blanket, the first sip of hot coffee in the morning.

A mystery is a perfect thing.

We do not know what will happen tomorrow. Trust is the most important thing. It helps you stay grounded, knowing you are guided where you need to be.

Embrace the unknown, the sparkles on the trail, and the knowledge that being who you are is your destiny. When you are your true self, you can conquer any obstacle that comes your way.

Intuition is a grand gift. Use it with wild abandon, and you will never be led astray.

Sometimes, we let fear overtake us. However, if you choose trust instead, you will find your way.

Forgive yourself if you embrace fear from time to time. It is bound to creep up out of the shadows to greet you. Just say hello, and let it go. Fear cannot stop you; only you can stop yourself.

We are here inside, watching, waiting, and knowing you are amazing. There is never room for doubt, fear, or obstacles from our viewpoint. We do not join you there. We wait until you have cleared those issues and are ready to start anew.

It is a beautiful day every day from where we stand. We love to watch you grow as a human being. You are loving, kind, and giving.

With love,
Your Inner Being

Dear Human Being,

When you set an intention with all of your heart, there is no doubt you will achieve it. It is a beautiful day when you believe in yourself.

We can show you how you can experience and bring joy to the world.

With big goals, you show you can perform miracles here on Earth. Something may seem impossible, but we know you can do it.

There are no limitations here.

The only obstacles are the ones we perceive. It may seem as if the world is solid and permanent. Yet, amazing things happen that are difficult for humans to explain. We are just waking up to our full potential.

This is the most exciting thing about being on Earth right now. If you are reading this, you were called to be here at this specific time to create joy, peace, and understanding. It may not seem like you can do this, but you can.

Activities you do for work or in your free time where the moments pass by quickly are your strengths. Use those to go for your dreams in life.

For example, if you love to write, sing, paint, or ride a skateboard-spend a lot of time doing those activities. Every chance you have, practice your unique art.

This is your way of performing miracles. By doing what you love, you show others it is okay to be themselves. Your examples move everyone forward.

Never think what you are doing is minuscule. It is enormous! When you love what you do, even for five minutes a day, you are making progress!

From our perspective, every step forward is monumental. We clap and cheer when we see you doing more each day. It is the best feeling from our viewpoint.

We observe you from above, knowing you are making progress.

Keep up on your trail. Put one foot in front of the other. No act is too small to count. If you see others doing more than you, cheer for them. They are only visible to you because you can go that far.

Write down your dreams, say them out loud, and declare to yourself you will go for them. When you do this, you cast a spell upon yourself. It is magic meant to propel you forward with action.

Act upon your inspiration, and you will succeed. If you are not inspired, rest and let go. Taking time out is not quitting. It is simply honoring where you are on the path and learning to breathe through it.

We admire you for all you have come here to do. It is an enormous feat to wake up with conviction and love. Thank you for all you do for your soul family.

With enormous love,
Your Inner Being

Dear Human Being,

You are such a loving person.

When you love with all your heart, it can sometimes hurt when someone close to you needs space to grow. It does not mean you did anything wrong.

They need room to spread their wings and fly. You have had times in your life like this. Moments where you needed time to find yourself.

Human beings are here to go through expansion.

At this time, it is happening at a quicker rate than in the past. We are all finding our way on the path at the same time. That is why it can sometimes be disorienting.

Yet, if you let go of what you expect others to be, they can grow. You will expand your being at the same time and for different reasons. You come together again and share your experiences of that time.

The most important thing we can share with you now is to trust.

Allow your intuition and heart center to guide you. Seeing someone become themselves is the greatest gift you can receive, even at a distance.

Everyone has a different timeline and way of expanding their heart, spirit and being. Love other humans as they grow.

Let them know they are loved no matter what. They can communicate, and they will be loved. They can go their own way and be loved. They are loved. Period.

In this way, we honor their evolving form as human beings, and we honor ourselves.

There is no wrong way to love in this case. As long as they know they can reach out if they want, that is all that is needed.

You see how beautiful and valuable they are just by being themselves.

What a gift!

It is a privilege to witness someone trusting themselves. Smile and know everything is okay. Before going home to a soul family, they will learn so much.

It is why you are here on Earth, to see others learn and to learn yourself. Once those lessons are learned, you expand, just like the universe.

We are all tiny fragments of spirit or source, finding our way in this world. Thank you for growing your heart one day at a time, no matter what.

You are always up for the challenge, come what may.

We love to see everyone reach goals, whatever path they choose. No matter what route you choose, it is always meant for you!

With love,
Your Inner Being

DEAR HUMAN BEING,

A feeling of being overwhelmed can wash over you at times. It is a natural part of being a human here on Earth. You were meant to make lofty goals, care for your loved ones, and hang on to each moment as if it were the last.

If you feel overwhelmed, reach for a place of calm within you. It is where we reside.

When your mind and body are spinning out of control, trying to check things off of lists, we wait beside you, holding a loving space for you.

This is a place of peace, love, and inner tranquility.

Sometimes, it may seem like it disappeared and was replaced by worry, tasks, and busy times. Yet, it lingers there, awaiting you with a candle of love.

We swaddle you in a warm blanket of eternal knowing. We know you may not accomplish everything in this lifetime, and nobody does. It is not about finishing everything. It is about having experiences while you are alive.

Have moments where you face your fears, love someone with all your heart, or grieve the loss of a loved one. Those are the moments that matter above all.

When a day feels like a swirling storm of constant activity, follow us to the refuge within. We will be there with a way to comfort you. Our love is like a warm cup of tea you can hold tight. It envelops you with care when you most need it.

We welcome you into the present moment, where everything you seek resides.

Sit down in a comfortable space and notice you are alive.

You can feel a deep breath coming through your lungs, showing you life. It is a miracle you are here, in this body, able to do all you do for yourself and others.

Stay in this moment for as long as you need. It will help you focus when the lists seem to take over.

The overwhelm will subside in time, and you will find yourself at peace, knowing all is well at every moment, even if you do not finish your tasks.

It will all be there tomorrow or in the next lifetime. Everyone leaves to go back to a soul family with things left undone. Choose the work that brings you the most joy and leave the rest behind. That choice will make your heart sing and bring others happiness.

When you choose to be in the present, we do a little happy dance. "They've got it!" We cheer out loud. You may not hear us, but we celebrate with you as you learn to take in everything within the flow of life.

What a beautiful journey it is to understand the universe in each person.

From where we stand, we hold you in love,

Your Inner Being

Dear Human Being,

Slowing down is a beautiful way to be. We love to see you take things easy and enjoy the process. The journey is what you are here for.

Often, humans forget that part.

You think it is all about the achievements or the metrics of life. It is the opposite of where we stand. Every time you develop a new relationship with time, you discover you always have enough of it to do what you please.

Remind yourself that there is always time for joy. This simple fact changes everything.

Leave a note where you will see it often that says:

"*I have plenty of time to do everything I need today.*" It will change your life.

Our mindset about time is a significant factor in how we live. When we think we are time-starved, we are. When we focus on having plenty of time, we do.

It seems miraculous, but it is only a change in our perspective.

From where we stand, time goes on forever. We understand it does not seem that way from your view. However, know that you are an eternal being. You may not have eternity in this particular life, yet you have all the time with your soul family.

Yes, the time you spend here on Earth is precious and fleeting compared to your time in the universe. However, it is worth slowing down because you will enjoy each moment more.

When you see the world with new eyes, as though time did not exist, you will find everything has a sparkle and air of beauty to it. You can stop and observe your life and see the infinite possibilities unfolding.

It is what we are here to present to you. A new way of looking at things.

We are so very proud of how far you have come in this life in all ways. It does not mean you do not have more to learn, but it is the process that is beautiful.

Learn through your mistakes, and you will become someone who uses your time wisely. You will no longer worry or spend energy thinking about time because you are in the flow. It is a state in which everything swirls around you, as if in suspended animation, full of joy.

What a magical world we all live in. You came here to experience everything, including being confused about time. It is natural and part of your experience.

Once in a while, you will still feel pressed for time.

When that happens, look at your note. Meditate for at least five minutes and slow down time for a while. Then, you will see there is no rush. Things will always work out as they are meant to.

Your role here on Earth is to fulfill your destiny. You will do that in good time.

With love,
Your Inner Being

Dear Human Being,

It is beautiful to see you enjoying life at every moment. Even activities like grocery shopping can bring so much joy.

If you stop to notice the abundance of the universe. It is all there on the shelves!

Today, you stopped by a unique store. It gave you so many memories. We were there to revel along with you. What a moment!

It is so much fun to enjoy everything you do. Life does not have to be mundane and monotonous. You can take pleasure in noticing the sights, sounds, smells, and a touch of each thing around you.

The beauty of a store is you can observe for free. You can marvel at all the cooking tools, even if you decide you do not need them. Imagine the chef buying a special apron. They are proud to cook for their guests tonight.

What a feeling of happiness it brings to take notice of the variety of objects around us. How was it invented? By whom?

It is a marvelous world here on Earth.

We are lucky to live in a place full of so much to see and do. There are never limits to what we can experience. The only limits we encounter are the ones we put in place.

We love to see you smile as you go through the aisles. Even the cleaning area can bring joy. Think about the ability to have a home or a business to clean. It is an honor.

It is beautiful to be grateful for the things we can do. To go shopping means you have mobility. You can push the cart from aisle to aisle without discomfort.

You can see the variety of produce and products laid out neatly on the shelves with your precious eyes. It is possible to hear the cashier ringing up your purchase. So often, we take these abilities for granted.

Know that you have everything you need to appreciate your life today. Even a single trip to the store can help you realize how much you have.

The love surrounding you is infinite, just like the number of items in a store. It seems to go on forever. The flavors of coffee syrups alone are mind-boggling.

Think of the universe expanding just like everything offered in an infinite store. That is what is available to you. You have no limits.

You can expand by opening up your imagination and changing your perspective on life. Allow yourself to see what is out there for you. The universe always wants the best for you, just like we do. We cheer on your every smile. It is a gift for all times.

We send you infinite joy just as you feel it in your heart. Thank you for being alive right now.

With love,

Your Inner Being

Dear Human Being,

It is wondrous how your days are filled with activities sparked by your desire and curiosity. You can be interested in everything from organizing a closet to improving your writing skills.

We love to see you follow the trail to bliss.

Did you know we put the little sparkles and breadcrumbs upon your trail? It is so much fun we can barely contain ourselves.

To see you moving about your day with purpose and joy is infectious. Never doubt following your heart in any situation. Activities that may seem like a waste of time from the outside never are. Each action you take towards feeling happiness is productive for your soul.

There is no wasted action.

Hear us when we say this: Following your impulses toward what you love to do is the key to everything. It is the only reason you came here.

Those are the beautiful moments in life, and they are the spark within your heart.

Receiving a message or impulse from us means that you are being led to something more you need to do. Until your time is up here on Earth, you will be guided every step of the way.

We guide you by putting things in your path that you love. When you feel like doing something, go forward! By all means, take some time to do something with joy. It is your birthright.

If you feel like redecorating and painting stars on the ceiling, do not hesitate!

Each thing you choose to do is another step along the journey you chose when you came here. Think about it like a star map. Finding your way means that you must follow that feeling in your heart. When you do, you will always be in the right place.

There is never a failure or a misstep. It may seem that way, but you were meant to learn from those experiences. Humans learn through trial and error.

We most like to nudge. However, sometimes, we push harder if we do not understand. Pay close attention to how you feel in your emotions. Those tell you so much about your path here on Earth.

If something does not feel right, do not go forward.

We are here to guide you through your feelings, those longings in your heart, and the joy you feel while doing something you love.

With love and joy,

Your Inner Being

Dear Human Being,

Working with determination is a gift.

Today, you found the focus to work with joy on a project. When you give yourself over to work you love, it shows. You can put your heart and soul into it.

It is when you shine, and sparks fly around your workspace. You may not see it, but we do. Those are remnants of the stars you came from.

All beings came from the stars, and the brightest ones cause a ripple effect here on Earth. You can radiate a glow through the work you do every day.

What a beautiful opportunity to wake up each day and face your upcoming work with a joyful heart. This work not only sustains you, but it also nourishes you with love and fortitude. When you think you cannot carry on, do you find more energy from within?

At the same time, guard and care for your talents and gifts. They are the treasure within you.

You are responsible for spreading a message of love. You do that through whatever craft you choose. At times, you are compensated for your work with money. Other times, you receive the love and admiration of others.

Both are equally valuable in your heart.

When your outside needs are met, you can give more of your talents for the benefit of all. Giving is the secret to abundance. When you have what you need, you let go of the rest for free.

Do not be afraid to give as much as you can. There can never be enough love in this world. We all need it now more than ever.

Love comes from many sources. It can come from a poem you write, a song you sing, or a pie you bake. As long as it is created with loving energy, it will change the person who receives it.

Often, you think what you do is small or insignificant, but it creates so much beauty in the world. Never doubt what you do matters!

What a beautiful opportunity it is to be a creator!

Each human is capable of creating. Especially in the age of technology, everything is possible. We love to see the infinite choices guiding you every day.

When you wake up and see the first light of day, remind yourself you create miracles. Say to yourself: "*I am a creator. Today, I will create something that matters.*"

It might be challenging to speak in such a tone to yourself, but you will understand the truth of these words in time. We have known them all along.

We thank you for your beautiful service just by being yourself.

With love to you always,

Your Inner Being

Dear Human Being,

It hurts to your core when you are let go from a job or a contract. We know it feels as if the world has crumbled all around you. You feel utterly lost. Forsaken.

Let yourself feel the emotions, and allow the tears to fall.

You are not broken. In fact, you are better than ever. The experience will guide you to something you have not considered before.

As you feel the pain drift away, a world can open up. Something not working out is a beacon to reach out and try something new. The universe calls you to pick up the pieces and try again.

Take a nature walk and let the soft wind caress your being into an inner knowing. We know what you came here to do, but sometimes humans forget. These difficult wake-up calls are a signal to your soul. Each one calls you to take action.

Before you set out on a new journey, let yourself feel the pain. We are here to comfort and console you. It is not your fault. Some opportunities in life are meant to be short-term experiences.

As you work through your emotions, know it is a grieving process. When this job came to you, it felt like fresh air, a door opening, the world knocking for you to answer. Yet, when it is taken from you, it can feel like rejection.

Do not hold on to the pain for too long. There is a specific reason for the loss.

You may not see it right away, but we do. We will continue to lead and nudge you in the right direction until you find it. Sit quietly with yourself, and you will know instantly. You will feel it in your body as a sensation. Then, it will surround your being with a deep knowing.

Sometimes, humans must go through pain or loss before they wake up to their true purpose. It was there all along, but they did not see it.

We can always sense your innate gifts. Each soul is given one before coming to Earth. You will keep exploring jobs, careers, businesses, and callings until you find it locked away in your heart. Do not let the pain of losing a job take over your days. You are meant for higher things.

Every soul sent here must let the music out of their heart for everyone to hear it.

If you keep your gift only for yourself, you are doing a disservice to humanity. Do not let that happen. We are holding space for you at every moment. We have all the time in the world. We know you have it in you.

We share these words: You are precious beyond measure.

If we could describe your soul's gift, it would be in a golden box surrounded by diamonds of all colors. It is locked, but you hold the key. Own this opportunity to unlock it and give away the contents, one day at a time. That is what your gift is for.

We know you are always capable of giving so much more. In return, you will receive the abundance of the universe. Your beautiful soul can capture light and shine it back at everyone here.

Thank you for working through the pain and coming to the other side.

With eternal love,

Your Inner Being.

Dear Human Being,

It may feel that you are alone. Yet, we reside within you to let you know you are loved. Sometimes, we know you need to hear this message. Some days are more challenging than others.

Humans are here to feel a full range of emotions.

When you accomplish something of significance, you feel elated and go out to celebrate. When there is a defect, you may feel like hiding. You want to go away and not come out again. It feels like darkness within your soul.

You may wonder why you came here, why you are needed. Do you have anything to offer your fellow human beings? It may seem like a futile effort to try once again. Sometimes, you are knocked down repeatedly. What is the point?

Withstanding the pain makes you stronger. If we did not think you could handle it, you would have stayed home with your soul family forever.

Yet, you chose to come here. You were chosen for something beyond your comprehension. You may see a small inkling of what it might be. Then, you may be distracted by trying to do something practical. We understand your confusion.

Life on Earth is a constant journey of ups and downs. Humans always want consistency and routine. However, if you do not get out of your comfort zone, you cannot grow. It is like trying to cage a tree. It cannot spread its branches toward the light.

Everything does not work out forever. Life has to flow like a river, curving and bending.

When you choose to grow through the changes, you will find joy. If you were overtired doing the job you lost, it allows you more time to dedicate to things that matter to you.

The universe is calling you to awaken.

An example is when you train your body in something like weight lifting or yoga, you challenge your muscles. They have to break down before they can build up. It is the same with your being. If you stay static every moment, you cannot grow and flourish.

When you choose growth over staying the same, you decide to come out of the shadows. You do not belong in the darkness where it may feel safe. Being out in the light may feel scary, but it is the only choice to become who you are.

Only we know what is on your soul contract.

Yet, you see a little glimmer of the contents every day. Each time you do something close to your heart, it is something written there. Doesn't that feel amazing?

Let yourself be guided by your feelings; you will know what direction to choose. It is all within your spirit. Let it out, allow it to soar freely, and it will beckon you to follow.

If you feel afraid to continue, do not give in to that fear. Change shows you the way forward. Sometimes, the only way up the mountain is the steep, rocky path. It may seem precarious, but it will hold you softly as you climb. Let your pain propel you to new heights. It is the push you need to get you going in the right direction.

With great love,

Your Inner Being

Dear Human Being,

If you mourn the loss of those who used to be close to you, never fear. Try to keep the doors of your heart open, but you may not match their energy.

Sometimes, our paths in life diverge.

Your beliefs about how the world works and theirs do not mesh. It does not mean you are a terrible person. The opposite is true. You hold yourself with love, and you give the same to others.

They may not be capable of loving you in the same way.

Just because they may not understand who you are does not mean they do not love you. It can be confusing and highly emotional. It was meant to be a part of your journey.

When there is difficulty in a relationship, it means there is hidden pain. Pain needs to be processed so that it can be let go. If it sits there, it is like stagnant water and does not flow away.

We can carry pain from one generation to the next. You are the one to stop the cycle. It may mean spending far less time with those that cause you pain.

You can choose to love them in your own way. It is not an easy choice. Sometimes, it is easier to try to have a close relationship with them and always agree. Yet, you cannot live an authentic life like this. You must be true to yourself and allow time and space to take over so that you can grow.

Personal growth sometimes happens through emotionally challenging circumstances. At times, you will not know what to do. In this case, trust your heart.

When you take time to sit with your heart, it will tell you what is best. Let go as much as you can.

It hurts to let go. To decide you are worth more time and effort. You cannot expect all the love to come from others. It must come from you.

You are the source of all the love you need.

The love inside your inner being is housed there for days when it feels like the world is breaking away. Reach inside and let the loving comfort you. It can shelter you from the storm while you heal.

Once your spirit feels new, you will be ready to step into the light and show the world your improved self. It is okay to let go.

We can love someone and not be in constant contact with them. If we repeatedly let the pain fester, we cannot be there for others. If you have children, it is best to let them move forward.

Allow yourself to grow, mature, and become who you were meant to be.

Send them love in a prayer, a letter, a call, or whatever feels right to you. There will always be love between you. It may not be perfect, but it is there.

With love always,
Your Inner Being

Dear Human Being,

When you choose to shine, the world sparkles with you! It gives us great joy to see you loving what is.

Isn't it beautiful how life is always working out for you, even if it does not seem like it? When you slow down and simplify, the best things come to you as if by magic.

Let us let you in on a little secret:

We are always here, waiting to sprinkle some magic upon your life. We wait for the moment in which we feel the most joy. We wish there were a way we could give you a big hug in the times you are low, but we have to wait until the pain subsides.

We have to allow you to feel all your emotions.

As a light being, you can sparkle most when you choose to do things that light you up.

What you choose may be different than someone else. It is okay. Know that you are loved as you are. We would not want it any other way. The universe created you, sprinkling in the perfect mix of stardust.

Shine on in whatever way feels best to you. You know exactly how to do that. Look within your heart where we reside. It is a place of great beauty, covered in love.

Choosing yourself does not mean forsaking others. It means you will be there for them and show them the best path. Sometimes, allowing others to find their way is the most loving thing you can do.

Often, you think you need to stay in the shadows for others to find you acceptable. That is far from the truth. The truth is, the more you share your life, the more you lift up others. It is the way of the world. Everyone has their own path to walk down. If you intervene too much, you may unknowingly place obstacles in the way.

Radiate in your light, and lift others if they ask you for help.

You will know your true calling by how it feels deep in your heart. If it feels correct, we are speaking directly to you. It is a beautiful gift to connect with your inner being, and we appreciate you for all you are at every moment.

We are grateful you are here, and we partner with you to create a beautiful world for everyone to live in. At this moment in time, the Earth is going through massive changes.

You are part of a new planet, an age of becoming yourself.

Far from selfish, you came to love yourself as an example of how to love others. When everyone sees your radiant, loving light, they will want to become that themselves.

Keep your light shining steadily, and more people will show up. You have been standing in the dark for so long. It can feel scary to step out into the sunshine. Yet, it is your birthright to be there. You are among the stars of the world, ready to provide loving energy to everyone who seeks it.

We love who you are,
Your Inner Being

Dear Human Being,

Sometimes, it feels as if you cannot slow down. You are moving quickly through your day, not noticing what is happening around you. The pace feels too fast.

We are here waiting for you to notice everything happens as it should. There is no need to hurry or run. Things will always be waiting for you. While it is paramount to always share your gifts, there is a time and place for everything.

If it feels as if tasks are mounting, and you feel the pressure of the world upon you, slow down.

It may feel counterproductive at the time, but slowing down does wonders for your spirit. Sit down, breathe, and relax. Time can slow down if you let it. Then, you can write a list of all your tasks. Leave some up to the universe to do and decide. They may not be paramount to do right now.

In a world where everything seems pressing, rarely anything is worth worrying about. When you focus on worry, things seem to amplify in importance. Yet, if you take a moment to check your list, not everything must be done now.

Take time to fit into your list. What speaks to you most? What can you let go of? What excites you?

These are tips that are rarely talked about. It seems everyone is trying to "hack" their productivity and time. There is no need for that. Everything will wait for you in the next life.

That is the key to life. You came here to learn life lessons and teach others. You are a beautiful, capable, and loving teacher. Anything else you do is extra. How does that feel? We bet it feels like an enormous weight has been lifted off your shoulders, right?

You can breathe easily. Each lesson you are here to learn adds to the light. A loving being like yourself is a joy.

Even when you feel overwhelmed, there is a blessing inside the chaos. It means you are in charge of so much goodness. It can be mistaken for work. We smile and laugh at this. We are here to assist you with anything you may need.

Do not be afraid to ask for help, for signs and signals along your path. We will provide them for you, but you must stay connected to us, your inner being. You can do that by slowing down, breathing, walking outside, or meditating. It is all within you. That is where we and the treasure lie.

You are a breathing treasure, alive with possibility. Your life is your lesson.

Tapping into yourself by slowing down allows you to access more of your gifts directly.

To unwrap them, you must slow your pace. A slow breath helps you center your being so that you can hear our faint whispers to your heart. We are always joyful when you listen. We never shout but use a soft, loving voice to guide you through your day. You may capture it more when you slow down.

It is with great love that we serve you today and every day. Thank you for being who you are. You light up the world.

With all of our love,
Your Inner Being

Dear Human Being,

When someone close to you is in pain, it hurts you. You are empathetic, and you feel everything around you. It can be a great gift, but it can be challenging.

As much as you want to help others, you must maintain positive energy. If you do, you will be a calming influence on everyone around you. Fear not, as those around you benefit more if you focus on your happiness.

We know it seems as if joining them in their pain and anguish will help them, but it does not.

That is why we always maintain ourselves in joy. We need to be here for you, to show you the way so that you may help others on the path. It is the way of the world.

Of course, if sorrow comes up, cry and let the tears fall down your face. They cleanse and heal you so you may move forward. Yet, wallowing in the pain will not help. When you have expressed your emotions, you can keep walking down the road leading you to the truth.

When you remain steady for others, they will see the way.

Allow them to evolve and grow at their own pace, no matter their confusion. You must stop shaking and wavering where you stand. Remain strong, and plant yourself on the Earth like a strong tree with deep roots.

Your roots are your faith, trust, and creativity. They will carry you far down the path to loving yourself. It is not a selfish act to find your own way in the world. When you do, and you are firmly planted, you provide an example to others.

When you grow and sparkle, others are attracted to your brightness. It creates a beautiful world: one person at a time. You make a difference just by being alive and sharing your experiences in a way nobody else can. If you share your whole heart, you create light.

If someone you love is in pain, reach out to them with your voice, words, and prayers. Lighting a candle and sharing your hopes for them is a beautiful act of kindness. That way, we can join you in your quest to help them find their way.

They can find the flicker of light in the impending darkness. You can be that glimmer of hope for them. Hold your lantern of life steady. Do not let it shake or waver with fear or sorrow. We are here to help hold it for you.

Your loved one also has a connection to us.

Take deep comfort in knowing they have a direct line to the source.

They may not know how to tap into it yet, but that is why you are there. When you share your creative solutions, you will help them find their own way.

The world is beautiful, imperfect, and whole all at the same time. Like crystals growing upon a rock, some shine bright, and some are just below the surface, waiting to emerge when the time is right. So it is with your loved one. They may need a tap to set them free. We all have the tools within us to access that universal spirit.

With great love for you and everyone,
Your Inner Being

Dear Human Being,

Some days, you may feel like you have too many ideas and little time. We understand this very well from the human perspective.

From the spiritual view, there is always more than enough time, as we are eternal beings. It may not seem like you will be around forever, but that is who you are. You came from a soul family, meant to live several lifetimes in service before returning to the non-physical world.

The physical world here on Earth is the most challenging. Yet, it provides the most opportunities for growth and learning out of all the worlds you could be sent to.

We tell you to embrace each day anew.

When you have an idea, run with it. Create what you desire and never look back. If it is not perfect, do it anyway. Others are there to inspire you. If you see someone creating something beautiful, give it a try yourself. You may be surprised by the results.

When you test out new skills and go down new avenues of exploration, we are giddy with delight. It is as if we get to explore these new things with you. What an adventure!

If you have art supplies, a camera, design software, dance shoes, an instrument, a pen, a pencil, or some paper, they are calling to you. Reach out to touch and play with the settings, the lighting, the rhythm, and more. Everything is here for your joy.

Somehow, your society beckons you to be realistic. Settle down. Find a job. Do the same thing forever.

We do not hold you to these standards. During this glorious time on Earth, it is time to explore, change, and love who you are. Do not remain static. Many do this, but there is no joy in their hearts. Listen to your spirit calling you to be creative with your life. This can take so many forms.

Do not be afraid to make mistakes when you tap into your creativity. Often, they lead you further down the path we are excited for you to take. Sometimes, they are even joyful accidents, ready to take over your creative spirit.

We smile brightly within you when you consider picking up that camera again; when the impulse comes to make a video, we are delighted. Look upon all those making a living doing what each one loves. Some have a channel where they play games, talk about them, and earn money. What fun!

In this age, the sky is the limit. It will continue to expand, just like the universe.

There are no limits if you allow yourself the space, time, and love to create. Yes, we mentioned love. It is time for you to expand and grow on this Earth plane. When you love yourself without a doubt, you will skyrocket to the top.

What a joyful day it is when you choose yourself!

It is a day we hoped would always come. We whisper softly, so sometimes, to hear us, you must repeat experiences many times. If you keep going down the path of overwhelm, we may pull you away for a while. Then, you can come back to your true creative self.

You are a precious gem, taking time to develop and grow your sparkly self.

With great love,
Your Inner Being

Dear Human Being,

Your pace of work may be different from others. Do not despair or worry. Each human has a different path in life and moves as needed to fulfill their purpose in life.

While it may seem like you are not productive some days, days of resting, observing, or doing other tasks are just as important as what you deem "work." Putting things in order in your home is just as valuable as producing art.

Each being has a certain amount of energy to spend each day. Some can go fast, doing many tasks while ignoring others. Yet others need to have an orderly space to start their work.

We are here to support you through it.

Find your own rhythm and pace in life, and embrace it with all your heart. You will be glad you did. Once you find the life balance best suited to you, you will know it. Your body will feel rested and ready to work when it is time, and your mind will quiet, knowing you have everything in order.

There are also seasons in life. If you follow the ways of nature, you will find great joy. Take time to count your blessings in the winter, and slow down to celebrate the season.

While you must show up consistently for your creative work, you also need time for fun. Pay attention to how you feel emotionally and physically. Those will be your clues. We will send you signals in many ways when you must slow down. You will feel the impulse to do more activities that bring you joy. Do them, and worry less.

Let go of the notion of constantly doing things.

It is not the way of the world, although society around you applauds it. We assure you that going with the flow of everything around you and with what feels right is best.

We smile when you are in the flow. Those are the moments when you do your creative work, and everything around you dances with light and joy. Those are the minutes that tick away on the clock without a care. Reach for more experiences like this.

Do not fret that some others appear to be doing more than you. You do not know their pace or ideal work setting. Only focus on what works best for you. That is the key to enjoying your work life as much as your personal one.

They should meld together just like the creation of a beautiful sculpture made of clay. Each day, you sculpt and carve your life, knowing what to add and take away. It is a joyful experience, as you are the artist of your life. You can choose to create whatever you wish on this Earth.

Your focus is one of the greatest gifts you are given by source energy. When you focus on things you love to do, everything else falls by the wayside. There is no need to worry.

We are always here to help you find your flow and center again. Tune into us through meditation or a quiet walk in nature. Watch what calls to you. You might see a feather on the ground or hear your favorite song on the radio. That is us, letting you know all is well and to continue on your path.

Never doubt those signs and that you are in the right place.

With great love for you,

Your Inner Being

DEAR HUMAN BEING,

It can often feel like you are not doing enough to get where you want to be. We want you to know your being is more important than your doing in life. Humans get caught in the trap of doing more.

We see the signs all around us. It is easy for you to doubt yourself and feel like you are not progressing enough. Yet, you are more than enough every day.

From our perspective, we see your dreams, hopes, and wishes with stars in your eyes.

Polish that sparkle every day by doing what you love. That is enough for the whole universe to see you from another galaxy. Do not ever doubt your sheer brilliance in this world.

Every day, you use your talents to share with others. Finding your flow is paramount to finding your passion and success.

If you do what feels best each day, you create a path for yourself and others to walk upon. You and others can also rest with ease when they feel tired.

Do not be afraid to share your vulnerabilities, weaknesses, and weariness. Those also make you strong. It lets others know they are not alone. When you desire something in your life: a fire is lit within, and we hold the match.

As you ignite and create masterpieces in your realm, we smile with the brilliance of a thousand suns.

Some days are for creating, others for pondering, and some for resting. You can do all three in one day or only one. We will be there to guide you as you choose what feels best. It may feel like a slow process, but we know it is all in divine time.

If you fall- we are here to pick you up from your exhausted state. We help you rest and regain your forces to spread love.

That is the meaning of love. Unconditional love is within you. It helps when you feel on top of the world and squeezes you extra tight with a hug when you are down.

Everyone needs this support, as their souls do not have a handy written manual telling them what to do here on Earth. You do not remember your plan to be here and what you would do. That is why we guide you in a silent, loving motion.

We are there when you smile at yourself in the mirror at morning's first light, knowing it will be a great day. We also console you when you are unsure of your next move. Some days, there is more clarity and some more confusion.

Yet, there is great beauty in the unknown.

It gives you the power to create each step, not knowing where it will lead, only that it feels right. Trust the feeling, as it is us. Every inkling you receive is a sign from the universe to keep going. It does not matter if you go fast or slow. Just keep going.

With great love,

LETTERS FROM YOUR INNER BEING

Your Inner Being

Dear Human Being,

There are days you may not feel the energy to accomplish your goals. As humans, you love to make to-do lists.

These lists are sometimes filled with non-urgent things. Yet, if it is on the list, it feels as if you must get it done immediately. We invite you to step back from your thoughts for a moment. Sit down, get quiet and let go.

When you do this, we can speak directly to you.

In the stillness, we can communicate with our souls. When you start to move again, you will become clear about your goals and ambitions.

Sometimes, you set out to do something because you think it is the right thing to do. However, how often does it feel exciting to do it? If you visualize it as a fantastic opportunity, go for it! On the other hand, if it feels dull and lifeless, leave it be.

There are moments in life when tasks appear on your list non-stop. You try to organize them and make new lists, and they keep popping up. We advise you to take some time off. It may seem like the worst idea of all. Yet, it is the best one.

When you slow down and get still, everything becomes clear. You can see down the path a little bit, and the fog lifts. It is like sitting down at your desk to write your masterpiece. All the pieces start to line up because your mind is not cluttered with other thoughts.

We encourage you to experiment with many different routines.

If you try many, you will find the best one for you. Some of you love to wake up early and face the day. Others encounter their creative genius after dark. Whatever it is for you, it is perfect.

You can learn from others and emulate them, but they are not you. Find your own habits and ways of being. Those will be the ones to carry you forward. You will find stability and comfort in them.

If a routine becomes stale, you can change it. Do not sit in worry and disdain for life. Re-arrange the furniture, take a walk, or change your schedule. We are here to support you in finding the best way to create.

Humans are beautiful creators. Yet, some do not allow themselves to create. They get stuck trying to do something that does not feel right, but they persist. Be quick to discard ways of being that do not feel comfortable. It leaves you time and energy to spend doing things you do enjoy. This lights up the whole world.

We have millennia of wisdom for you to tap into. It will help propel you forward even on the darkest of days. Do not fear anything; we are here to help light your way.

Routines, habits, and schedules are ways humans work on ordering their world so that they can find and follow their soul's path. Someone rarely finds it on their first try. Do not despair if it takes you many attempts. Even when you find something that works for you, it may need to change with time and circumstances. Your life is more like nature than it seems. Even with advances, life ebbs and flows, going around obstacles and becoming stuck along the way, just like a river does.

We love you at every moment,
Your Inner Being

DEAR HUMAN BEING,

It is beautiful to see you share with others. Your talents are a shining example of giving. When you create a community around your work, you can shine together.

Working together is more valuable than standing on a pedestal alone.

You will feel the love around you when you do what you love and support others' dreams. A situation where everyone wins is the best outcome.

There is always more than enough abundance for all. At this moment, the universe is expanding. It is like a balloon inflating without ever running out of air. Imagine your life ever-growing, just like the universe. It is a beautiful sight from where we stand.

The more you grow, change, and embrace who you are, the more will come to you. You do not have to push for it or make an enormous effort. Give yourself grace about where you stand. We will put everything into motion for you to succeed when you do what brings you joy.

When you do something that is not a match- it will not serve you or others.

For example, if you do something purely to earn money: and it is a tedious job, the universe will kick you out. It may be painful at the time, but it is because we know where you belong. You need to remain where you find the most light in your heart.

When your days glide by with a smile, we light up inside. We will keep you in a loving embrace of your soul.

What a glorious being you are!

You can create whatever you want with technology at your fingertips. Today is the day to seize the opportunity to make a masterpiece with your mind. We know sometimes thoughts can get in the way. Push them to the side and understand you have everything you need to create the life you want.

Use the power of your focus to put something beautiful out into the world. People need your talents to create a special love in the world that will solve many problems. Many times, solutions are simple.

We support you in every exploration you make. Listen for our whispers to guide you in the right direction. You will feel a calling to do more of what you love. Pay attention to that. Do not listen to the voice telling you that you are not enough. You are a powerful, incredible being. You came to this Earth to unite everyone in harmony.

Do not doubt your purpose is to send love out into the universe. It will shine on forever in a star.

The work you do today is paramount for everyone to thrive. Put out positive energy into the world right now; it will help us all move forward. Use every day to create this love inside you and transmute it into working with others. It will create a ripple effect that carries over into everyone's hearts.

When you focus on your strengths, you will fulfill your destiny here on Earth. Many souls here think they must do something grand to help humanity. Yet, being who you are is enough.

With great love,
Your Inner Being

Dear Human Being,

You are on the precipice of something spectacular! Each you inch closer to the edge of realizing your dreams. When you dare to dream, it unfolds right before your eyes.

Doubt is a dream crusher. Do not allow doubt to come near your precious thoughts and words. When it does, brush it away gently.

If you feel unsure, take a walk and give it some time. Over those moments, feelings will bubble to the surface. Those feelings are us communicating with you. If you feel a surge of joy about something, it is a sign to go for it.

Yet, if you do not feel very excited about it, it may be something you should let go of.

Focus on the good feelings bubbling up inside. It will help you move forward with something beautiful in your life. It is why you came here and what we continually help you with daily.

Once you sit down to create, you are growing and healing. You feel poised and ready to take the plunge into your deepest heart. It is there where the magic resides. Do not be afraid to delve deep into yourself to make discoveries.

Each day you will find more joy. As the excitement around an idea unfolds, we are there to sprinkle magic upon it. Our magic is found in that fluttering feeling in your stomach or the beginnings of a smile on your face.

Let your inner joy uplift you. Know that you can accomplish what feels best to you. Our best advice to you is to wait for the signs. You will understand how it feels. That may seem strange, but it is true.

Look for others who are creative like you. Find comfort in those willing to uplift you with positive words and deeds. You will find a community of humans like you, filled with joy and ready to move forward.

We are here like your life coordinator. We ensure everything you need dances around you like a perfectly orchestrated ballet. Sometimes the dance may be intense or dramatic, but those are just lessons you must learn along the way.

Our voice tells you: "All is well; you must trust in every step of the way."

When you put your faith and trust in life, it will return the favor. Be abundant, kind, and patient. Your rewards will come, and then you can share them with others. That is what you are here to do, to be in communion with all human beings to create a loving world.

Start with love, and everything follows. It is this message you must carry within your heart at all times. Stay faithful to it, and you will need nothing else.

With great love,
Your Inner Being

Dear Human Being,

The silence of the morning is the best time to connect with us, your inner being. We love the quiet moments of stillness before all activity starts. These are the minutes in which time seems to slow. You can focus on your breath in meditation and be in harmony with your true self.

Before any thoughts enter your mind or information clogs your joy, spend some quiet time with yourself.

It is there you will find all the answers you need. You may often feel you need more information to choose when it is within you, waiting to be discovered. Whenever you "know" you need to do something, that is our whisper.

We will not yell or knock you over, but we may sometimes say no to something that is not right for you. You have all the power to decide to do it anyway. Yet, if you do, something will seem off. Pay attention to those subtle feelings within you whenever you need to pick a direction in your life.

Knowing what feelings of joy spark you will help you move forward. Activities that flow easily are the ones to hold onto. Those are the ones that bring peace to your heart.

Success in something is not automatic. It is a slow, gradual unfolding of your life. Your path is winding and sometimes treacherous, but we will never let you fall into the valley below. We hold you steady with our joyful nudges to try something new daily.

The more you trust your inner knowing, the easier it will be to climb the mountain of life. You have all the tools you need to get there. Just focus and believe you can make it.

That focus comes from quiet time and meditation. Take some time out during breaks throughout the day to strengthen your connection by sitting quietly. Listen, and you will hear the rumblings of miracles starting to bubble into existence. It is with great joy we place them there for you to discover.

With great love,

LETTERS FROM YOUR INNER BEING

Your Inner Being

Dear Human Being,

When you show up for yourself, that is when the magic happens. Time and again, we see you put yourself last. Yet, if you give yourself love and time, miracles happen.

We feel a great love for you, infinite and vast.

This love can help you create whatever you desire in this lifetime. You only have to focus and believe. We know it can sound simplistic, but it is the truth. When the momentum of your life's work starts to build, it will swirl around you like a thousand suns.

There is always enough energy, time, and effort to create what you want. Believe this, and everything will follow.

We cannot describe the enormous joy we feel when you finally decide you are enough. You are more than enough to make your dreams happen.

Sometimes the results do not show up immediately, but they are right under the surface. They ripple and start to create waves that crash onto the ocean of your thoughts. The more you concentrate on them, the more fantastic they become.

Riding the wave of inspiration and enthusiasm is one of the greatest thrills in life.

It starts out as if you are given a single drop of water. Your thoughts create and shape something beautiful and new. In very little time, you see it growing into a flowing creek, then a river that leads to the ocean.

As you flow along, you may come upon sticks or stones in your way. You gently brush them aside and continue. Each object in your way teaches you a lesson that grows your thoughts, ideas, and experiences into something extraordinary.

During your journey, you may also experience rough waters. Those are called doubts. They sometimes surge and then mellow as you find your balance.

Once you are near the ocean, you are unstoppable. This place is meant for you. Guides will show up to help you along the most treacherous areas, assuring you of your strength. They, like us, feel great love for you and will give you the tools you need to make a lifetime of dreams come true.

Our excitement for you never wavers all along the way, from the drop to the ocean.

You have so much power, strength, and love inside you to carry you all the way. Listen to the whispers of guidance if you need a helping hand. We want you to find the momentum to carry out your mission here. It is of utmost importance that you never stop once you start. You may have temporary delays, but do not let them stop you from continuing your journey to the heart of who you are.

Each time you veer off course, we will send you a sign. At first, you may not recognize it. Yet, it will become apparent what you must do next. Sometimes you may feel these signs are too intense. Some of them may come in the form of losing an opportunity, but you will understand it was not a match for you.

Never fear, for we have your best interests at heart. You may try many different paths in life, but you will find yourself returning to the one that feels best.

With great love,
Your Inner Being

DEAR HUMAN BEING,

You are a guiding light for others to follow. Your shining heart will lead everyone to love. To shine your light, you must do work you love every day. It is not a singular effort but one done with a team.

When you invite others to work with you: your power will be brighter than the sun.

We support your every move. We do not interfere, and we only observe and encourage. You will know what to do. Follow the subtle signs and cues along the way.

Life is beautiful when we allow it to unfold. It is like a flower bud, slowly unfurling to reveal the beauty inside. It is who you are. Allow your life to flow and mature from moment to moment. Everything you see, hear, and experience is a message from the universe straight to your heart. Loving clues appear where you least expect them, from graffiti on the wall to something someone says to you.

The more you pay attention to these signs, the more your inner glow will show to the rest of the world. We speak directly to you through your outer world. We do not have an audible voice, but when you appreciate something, we are there.

How wonderful to notice every detail around you as if it were a symphony of love. Every glint of sunshine, every step you dance to, and the smile on your face are ways you know all is right in the world. Thank you for showing up every day to show the universe your work.

You never know who you will impact with your radiance. The more you shine, the more people will find love in their hearts. If you dim your words or actions and retreat into the shadows, the world will never know how bright you are. It is with great love that we support every move you make.

Every action you take leads to lessons. Those lessons show you other ways of being. Keep experimenting and become a scientist in your own life. That is the way of being with the world. We appreciate your every breath here on Earth. It is a joy to know you.

Believe it or not, we know everything in your soul contract. Before you came here, you created it to learn special lessons. It is a document sealed with love. Sometimes those lessons may seem overly painful. Yet, we know it will lead you to a loving place.

Each soul is unique and beautiful, just like a shining crystal. You reflect the light in each person's spirit. It is a priceless gift and the best one you can give others. Try lighting up the world with your unique smile. You never know how it will change someone's day.

Every time you have an idea, try it out. The spark to do something ignites a light in your soul. It is always a miracle if you trust it. Sometimes these actions can be small, but they impact the world. Thank you for the service you provide here on Earth. By learning your lessons and sharing them, you light up the world.

Your light burns bright like an eternal flame, and you are a beacon of hope. Like a lighthouse, you attract others to join you in your mission to create a better world. What joy and love that sparks within us as well. It is a success story!

Your love and heart are what fuels the Earth. They are the secret ingredients needed to bring us all to the next stage of evolution to become a peaceful place. Practice being loving and kind to everyone. We thank you for each smile, hug, and word of encouragement. You are loved.

With great love,
Your Inner Being

DEAR HUMAN BEING,

During the holidays, it can be a stressful time. Everyone adds more items to their to-do lists. It seems as if there are too many things to accomplish this season. At the same time, stay true to yourself, know your limits, and give yourself grace.

Doing what you love and what sounds fun are the keys to joy and happiness in your heart.

We love it when you take time out to enjoy life. Humans always think it is all about getting tasks done when it is really about how much joy you extract from the doing. If something is feeling heavy, take it off your list. You may return to it later, or you can decide to leave it off your list forever.

It is your choice, and when you have a chance to reflect upon it: you will enjoy letting go.

An exercise you can try is this:

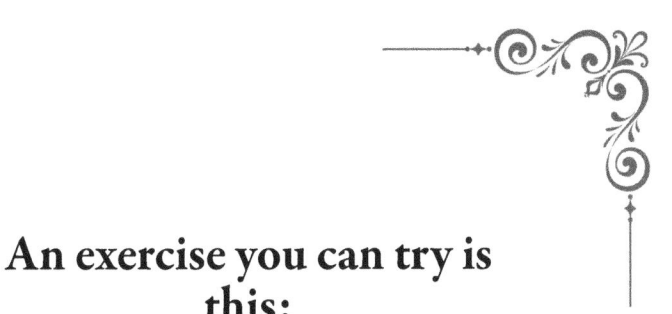

Make your favorite beverage like tea, coffee, juice, or hot chocolate.

Light a beautiful candle on your table.

Sit down with an index card or a piece of paper.

Write: What sounds fun?

Take a few moments to explore that question in your heart. What do you feel excited to do? What lights up your days?

Then, write one or two things you want to focus on this season.

It will help to slow down and center yourself for a few moments. This season is full of overwhelming, busy moments. It is paramount for human beings to rest and take care of themselves. They must realize their worth.

Know that you are loved no matter what you do. You could take days to accomplish a single thing, and we would cheer you on. You are a loving, light-filled being, and we love to see you do what makes you shine every day.

The traditional tasks of this season may not be what is correct for you right now, and that is okay.

It is of utmost importance that you tune into your intuition to solve any issues of feeling overwhelmed at this time. It is supposed to be peaceful, but this season can bring too much stress. When you feel lighter, you can do your best work.

We are always here to lift you up, take things off your list, and make your life bright. Your only job is to do something you love. We know it sounds too simple, but it is the way of the universe. This constantly expanding world of stars, planets, and galaxies is a world of abundance and joy. There is always more than enough for everyone. When you do your work with love, it flows into everything you accomplish.

As you decide on the best plan of action to best fit who you are as a beautiful human, we are here to support you. You do not have to do everything perfectly. You are perfect as you are. If you send gifts and write cards, that is the best choice. If you choose to lighten your load, we love you.

With great love,
Your Inner Being

DEAR HUMAN BEING,

Each time you create something, you put love into the world. We love to see you light up, sprinkling love everywhere you go. It is a pure delight to see you sparkle.

Shining bright is what you do best. You are a lightworker here to spread the good news that all is well at every moment.

It is with great joy that we support you every second.

When you make time for what you love, your whole being lights up like a Christmas tree. All the colors illuminate the path you walk on with love. It is with this joy that we cheer for you at every turn. Hooray! We shout and jump for joy as you cross another finish line in your life.

Each day is a special kind of race. It does not mean you need to rush or hurry. It only means that when you create something to put out into the world, it is like breaking the ribbon at the end of a marathon. Challenging yourself out of your comfort zone and creating is so beautiful. It is the moment we wait for each day.

What a loving, delightful being you are! We mean every word we say when we compliment you on your very existence. You are a brave soul to be here in the first place. It takes determination and tenacity to stay on this Earth.

At every moment, we prepare you for the race of your life. We put inspiration on your path and lead you to choices that will further your joy, and we applaud you when you choose to share with others. The instant you sleep, the ribbon is cut for the next day.

In the morning, when you meditate or spend some quiet time contemplating, you set the stage for the next race. By this analogy, we mean that you prepare yourself to do work that brings joy to yourself and others along the way. It is as if you run along, handing out flashlights to everyone you meet. You are spreading the light with your work.

It does not matter if you spend your days caring for children, writing software, or cleaning a building. It is the race toward joy that matters. Each calling is unique and meant for you. Go towards something you love the most. You will know what it is by how it feels.

What pure joy you are!

Imagine a cheering section so large you cannot fathom it. That is us every day, following you around. We wave around our ethereal pom-poms and create chants of encouragement. You must be quiet rather than turning up the volume.

We thank you for rising each morning to a new day because it means another 24 hours of your mission here on Earth. Every moment is paramount, even though it may seem mundane. Nothing could be further than the truth. Each second you are here, we are thrilled beyond belief.

Even when you return to your soul family, we will cheer you on as you decide on your next assignment. What happiness you bring to all whose lives you touch with your heart.

With love,
Your Inner Being

Dear Human Being,

We feel your pain at times. When you are human, your feelings come right to the surface. It feels as if your world is broken. You feel at fault, yet you must let others carry on.

Hold steady and know you are loved.

Allow your emotions to flow, yet know you are supported by us at every moment. You are loved beyond measure here in the spirit realm and much beyond. You do not remember your world before you arrived on Earth, but your mission was clear. Find the love in your heart for Earth.

What on the surface looked perfect in your family now feels like it shattered into a million pieces. There are illusions in this life. You can let go and know you will be okay. Everyone needs to find their own path in life. If you try to hold them together, they will not discover it.

You need to discover what is hidden deep in your heart. It is a treasure waiting for you to find it. Things need to break wide open so that we can grow.

Without growth, your human experience would not be complete. We wait for you to find your own way. We place clues for you to find and people to lead you where you need to go. Yet, you make the choices.

It is a beautiful world you live in. Every day you are alive and breathing here is a gift. Do not be unkind to yourself. You do the best you can every day with the tools in your heart. Use your spirit as a toolkit to help yourself and others.

They may not always understand you or your ways, but they love you.

Every relationship you have on this Earth is significant. Sometimes, you may feel unsure about how to communicate. We will lead you. When you have the intuition to use your words, express yourself. It is also okay to be silent sometimes. It does not mean you do not care. It only means you need to let your spirit rest for a while.

Allow yourself time to heal, grow, and discover who you are. Earth is the most challenging and rewarding place for a soul to be. Give yourself time and grace. You will find your way, dear heart.

Your sweet, delicate heart needs time to understand the ways of everyone. Not every human feels as deeply as you do. They may not comprehend your spirit and way of being. Yet, their modes of being are valid to them. It is a paradox of the world.

You aren't alone in your confusion. Especially on holidays, it can feel lonely without the gatherings that once were. You can go your way forward, spreading love as only you can. Those who capture your light are transformed forever. They know the way.

Follow those who light a candle for your heart. Many of you are starting to gather, and you will soon meet to create change on this planet. It will be a glorious day filled with love, and it will change everyone around you. Trust that you are in good hands.

Trust life. Your inner being loves you beyond time and space. It is a great love that never ends. Even when your time on Earth ends, we wait for you and your next mission.

Thank you for every second you are alive.

With great love,

Your Inner Being

DEAR HUMAN BEING,

Please know that it is okay to walk away. You will know when to leave if people and circumstances do not feed your spirit. In this life, it is best to be as loving as possible. Sometimes, that is better from a distance.

It may hurt your heart, but you will become stronger and more resilient. We see the light in you every day, even though you may only see embers that flicker on and off. It is a joy for us to see you gain strength. Remember that others often have to find their own way. If you interfere too much in their soul's development, it may slow them down.

If another person asks for assistance and you can help them, please do so. Yet, if they do not ask for help and it is not an emergency, leave space between you to heal.

Often, souls like you come into intense family situations.

You are meant to break a pattern in this family. It is your life lesson. It will be painful and confusing. It will hurt your whole spirit at times. Yet, you must move on, creating a more loving, inclusive, and relaxed place for your loved ones. It is your life's journey.

Listen to your intuition and gut feelings. Look around for signs. Whatever your heart calls you to do or not do is the correct action to take.

Holidays and special days like birthdays may be challenging to get through. Forge your way by sending love to everyone. It may be in a letter or a small gift. Each token of your love sends out ripples of kindness. You do not need to present or subject yourself to gatherings you do not wish to go to spread love.

Often, human beings confuse obligation with love. Do not worry if it happens to you a multitude of times.

Consider how you feel when around others. It is okay to love them exactly as they are but from far away. The space in between allows your soul to grow in different ways. Sometimes, this is interpreted as an unloving thing to do, but it is the most loving act you can accomplish.

Learning to let go is a way to allow two or more souls to grow and flourish. Without the separation, they grow stagnant, unable to learn powerful lessons.

A negative pattern, once interrupted, can create a ripple of joy in everyone's lives. At first, it may seem extremely painful, but it is the only way to move forward. Once you recognize a long line of pain in your family, you can stop it and let it go.

It is a beautiful, loving thing to do. You can still communicate with loved ones as you see fit, as your heart and space allow. Let them know they are cared for and loved. By loving yourself more and allowing this room to grow, you can fly and help others do the same. It is your life's work here on Earth.

Your soul chose to come here in these exact circumstances to further the development of Earth. Whatever happened is not your fault but the natural order of things given to you. You will see more beauty in it as the days pass.

Value those you hold dear. Do not judge others for their choices. They are doing the best they can with different lessons and missions.

With great love,

Your Inner Being

Dear Human Being,

Some days, your attention can scatter all over the place. It can happen because deep emotions are surfacing, or perhaps you are overwhelmed with holiday stress. No matter the cause, we invite you to focus only on what brings you joy during those times.

Even if you create something with a loving focus for five minutes, it is enough to bring a smile to your face. Know you are making progress in your world one moment at a time. It may not seem like very much, but small efforts add up.

Five hundred words written daily add to a book over a short period.

We are here to encourage and inspire you. It does not have to be perfect to be great. You do not need to finish everything at once. There is time to slow down and sit with your project.

When you sit down to create, even when times are busy, it means you are choosing yourself and your mission. Sometimes, you may give in and say you must do other activities. Every time you choose yourself, you put love into the world.

By reading these lines right now, you radiate your light.

Love, care, and sweetness go into everything you accomplish. It may be a journal entry, a quick sketch, or the bars of a melody. Whatever it is, create it now. The polish will come later; it is the diamond in the rough we want to see.

Every moment has its focus. Focus more on creating than other tasks. Those tasks will be there day and night, but your creativity has a time window each day. For some, it may be the mornings; others are night owls. Find your time to make a masterpiece and share it with the world. It is never too late.

You came into this world with love. The more you share, the more love you create. It is as simple as that. You are a creator of worlds. You may think you need power to do this, but it is not the case. With your light, you have everything you need right inside you.

The more you cast doubt aside, the more progress you will make on your dreams and goals. It is a day of joy when you say yes to being the creator you were born to be!

We all have access to the source of all creation, and as your inner being, we point you in the right direction. Sometimes, we have to help you remove distractions, such as shiny objects, so that you will work on your mission. We are sorry for the heartache it sometimes causes. We know you will understand in the end.

All the failures in your life point you toward what you are meant to do.

We walk the path daily with you, sometimes sprinkling in inspiration like a song, numbers, photos, and memories to delight you. Those sparks of joy catapult you into a storm of creativity. That is when we cheer you on the loudest. We may only sound like a whisper in your ear, but our voices are like those at a large stadium. We love to see you follow your path of creation.

We follow you daily, watching you create what you love. Listen to those little voices talking to you, encouraging you to take more steps. That is us. We are here to guide you to your loving home here on Earth. Thank you for allowing us to help you along the way. We know it is not always easy every day, but you will not regret trying.

With great love,
Your Inner Being

Dear Human Being,

It is a new year, and we are so excited for you! A change in the calendar brings humans an opportunity to try challenging things.

We invite you to look upon yourself with grace and compassion as you start this journey. At the start, everything seems perfect, exciting, and mesmerizing. Yet, there will be days of doubt. On those days, remember the first day you started with unbounded optimism.

That level of excitement is what we hold for you every day. Every second that the clock strikes, we admire you. There is never a day where we feel anything but love for you. So, as you go about your days and new routines, know our appreciation for your path knows no bounds.

We are like someone who lights a candle in the window for you every day and never allows it to extinguish. We will keep the flame lit for you so that you have the energy to do what your heart desires. Never stop working towards your dreams.

A new year gives you time to reflect, go inward, and review what matters most.

Here are some questions we want you to keep in mind when planning your goals and dreams for this new chapter in your life:

Does it feel fun to you?
Does it feel loving?
Does it feel like something you will sustain?

These three questions help you move forward by paying close attention to your feelings. So often, humans forget their inner compass or feelings when moving ahead with projects. Their sense of self is tied to accomplishing something, not how it feels. We urge you to pay more heed to your feelings about your actions.

It may not make sense, but it will make all the difference. When you feel love in your heart for a task, you will progress faster and find more joy in the process. Often, human beings are concerned only with the outcome of a path in life. Each step is paramount for you.

We appreciate every experiment you do in life and everything you try. No work is done in vain. You see, you came here with life lessons to learn. We ensure you stay on track. Sometimes, you may feel your path has swerved in a different direction. Do not fear.

Our love for you never wanes, and you are always protected upon your path.

It is with great joy that we celebrate you starting new goals, projects, and life choices in the new year. The time is now to ring in the person you have always been, a loving and shining example of you.

With each new experiment, you will see growth in who you are becoming. We watch for each new thing you learn and discover about yourself and the world along your path to greatness. Each human being is a seed of life, waiting for fertile ground to become a great tree of love. Giving all its strength to help humankind.

Every day, you water and nourish the seed within you to grow yourself. You are always perfect, steady, and beautiful along the way, no matter how many times you may stumble and fall. It is always meant to be.

With great love,
Your Inner Being.
Dear Human Being,

We know sometimes starting something new can be very frightening. It may feel like you do not have a solid foundation when you start. Yet, the whole world is waiting for you to show up more. Some people will be touched by your words and will stand in loving admiration for your art and wisdom.

Whatever it is that you create in this world and share with others, it is needed.

Right now, we stand at a divide in humankind. The light that you shine outward directly from your heart in the form of something beautiful is what will heal the world. It may seem strange to hear this because we think we must do something big to make a difference.

Just doing what you love can heal the whole planet. That is because every creative act causes a ripple effect. You never know what power your creativity has until you unleash it upon the world and watch it light up someone's life.

We appreciate you sharing your true feelings with the world. That is what we need right now, the authenticity of spirit. When you are true to who you are, your brightness amplifies. It radiates throughout the planet like a beacon of hope.

Never fear creating something. There is nothing to lose. In fact, there are so many tools right at your fingertips. A laptop and a smartphone can create beauty for all the world to see. There is no need for fancy or expensive equipment to share your gifts.

Use what you have at this very moment to create something unique and beautiful with the world. Share it as soon as you can. Do not worry if it is perfect. The more you share daily, the more your love will shine out to everyone who needs it.

We promise you that your creative effort is never in vain. You may not reap the benefits of it right away in a monetary sense. However, as you build your credibility and portfolio, others will take notice of your gifts and what you offer. Your light will be bright and irresistible.

We love to see you grow and flourish right where you are.

With great love,
Your Inner Being

Dear Human Being,

We know sometimes you feel fear even about doing creative and fun things. It can be scary to step out of what you deem safe. We are here to tell you it is always a good place to be.

Every day of your life is a new chance to experiment and become the person you were meant to be. The path reveals itself to you day by day. Your job is to feel into each moment and decide what feels best.

During our lives, we are told to do the sensible thing or something everyone else does. That thinking keeps you trapped in a loop, going in circles and dazed. To find your path- the cycle needs to stop. Stopping can feel disorienting, so that is why you often feel fear.

Yet, know that feeling it for only a moment and diving in is the way to go!

It is liberating to use that box of colors and paint the world around you. Know that it is one of the most exciting moments for us. We exclaim: "They've got it!"

We know it can be frustrating because we deliver very subtle signs. However, please know that we do so out of kindness and gentleness to you. Once you learn to pick up on these signals, life feels effortless.

Each time you pick up the paintbrush or do anything to create, you walk the path to your destiny. You never know who will feel awe when viewing your art or who will change their lives upon reading your book.

You will build momentum each day you choose yourself. Think of an act of creation like a bit of snow packed onto a snowball. Each day, it grows bigger on top of the mountain. One day, the ball starts to roll in your life. Run with it and discover who you are!

Become the creator you always knew you could be. We hold you in that light every second of the clock. What a joy it is to see your progress toward your dreams every time you choose to create. Each human being has an enormous capacity to love, share, and grow. Your growth takes off like a rocket when you keep going no matter what.

At first, you may have little feedback. Yet know that with each passing day, you will reach more people. Learn to support them, and you will grow into a supportive community.

You can achieve only so much. Together, you build a better world.

We are connected to you every step of the way. Even though it sometimes feels like you are doing your work alone, we are always there to guide you. We view you in the highest esteem, even at your lowest moments. We never think less of you and know you can accomplish anything.

Your work radiates energy others will find in their hearts. That is the energy that creates love in the world. Right now, it is paramount that humans find that energy and build upon it to form a sustainable planet for all to thrive.

We believe that sharing your gifts and talents as often as possible is the key to creating the world every one dreams about. It may not seem this way, but each moment you work on something you love, it will ripple its energy out to others. The love they feel in their souls then transfers to more people. It has an effect you may not see, but it will happen with your help.

With great love,
Your Inner Being.

DEAR HUMAN BEING,

There will be times in your life when you come upon resistance. It will feel like going upstream in a river with the strongest current you have ever experienced. We know it feels insurmountable.

We know once you do that which is in your heart, you will feel freedom within your spirit. Take the time to sit with the uncomfortable thoughts and actions. It will take a lot of strength and will, but you can do so much more than you can imagine.

We are aware that sometimes you are fearful of hurting the feelings of others, so you choose to stay small, hide in the shadows, and not let your light peek out. This non-action hinders your life and others who need your brilliance and emotional strength.

Do not doubt you can speak with your heart and be direct, firm, and loving with someone challenging. It may take effort and soul-searching, but we are confident it is within you.

When you share the truth and do not hide what you believe, your actions will be rewarded by the universe. We are waiting with joyful applause when you decide to do that task, speak your truth, or stand up to someone with a different opinion.

Not voicing who you are and what you believe in keeps you in the darkness.

As your inner guides, we always hold you in shimmering light, but you must choose to rise above the shadows. It will be a great day of celebration, happiness, and lightness when you decide to do something you have avoided until now. The pain of thinking of it will disappear into the clouds once you say yes to your soul.

We are waiting for you to share the truth inside your heart with everyone. Then you will come alive!

With great love,
Your Inner Being

Dear Human Being,

When you are growing and evolving as a human being, there will be some pain and discomfort. Those are signs that you are opening up about who you are. It is much like when you go to the gym regularly and feel the soreness in your muscles. It means you are getting stronger.

As you stretch out of your comfort zone, things may feel challenging. You may feel more fear than ever before. We are here to catch you if you stumble along the way. We love to see you put time and dedication into your dreams.

We are the voice that whispers: Keep going!

Some days, it may seem like there is no point in going up the long, steep hill of life. We are here to reassure you that once you open yourself to the journey and everything with it, connections will appear to help you.

If you stay on the path through the wind, rain, snow, hail, and sleet, you will find soul friendships to uplift you when you are down. We assist you in finding them so that you may continue with confidence. You are always loved.

Pay close attention to messages you receive from others. You will know in your heart the actions to take along the road to your life's mission. You were meant to shine bright and to carry your message wide and far.

We accompany you with every step you take. One foot in front of the other is the only way to accomplish goals. Some days, you may doubt you are progressing. Yet, sunshine is just around the corner. You are gaining strength with everything you do. As your confidence grows, so will your love for all.

You came here with a powerful love to give to everyone on Earth. Some are easy to give to, and others more challenging. That is why you must not ever give up.

When you feel weak, lean on us. We are the balm for your soul. Take a rest on our shoulders, and let us carry you to a place of rest for a while. After your spirit is renewed, you may continue your journey. On Earth, it is known as compassion for yourself.

Give yourself grace along the path and gain wisdom on the way to greatness. There is no perfection, only progress toward that which you seek.

It is a beautiful thing to fail. It means you have learned a life lesson to carry you forward. Reflect on your failures and give thanks. They are the keys to becoming who you are. Without stumbling blocks, we would not grow.

Know that you are in a growth phase if you feel uncomfortable and unsure. It only means that illusions that once held you up in life are dissolving all around you. You may feel a little unstable, but it is because you are evolving.

We are excited for you at this very moment. You are on the precipice of something extraordinary! Hold tight and enjoy the ride of your life at this time. We inspire you to continue your work and spread your light and love.

With great love,
Your Inner Being

DEAR HUMAN BEING,

Today, we want to congratulate you on all you do to spread light and help others. No act is too small to notice. Helping those you live with is a beautiful way to share kindness with the world.

When you do things with love, we notice.

Our appreciation is like the joyful feeling you get when you are delighted with life. It is the smile on your face when your favorite song comes on the radio. It is happiness bubbling up in your spirit.

Making a meal for others with care is one example. The love you pour into your preparations creates energy to fuel the people you feed. Everything around you is energy. It is your choice to imbue it with positivity.

Create the light for all to feel connected to. You do that through your daily activities. You may not think that doing laundry or hugging your child is monumental. Your love radiates through everything you do.

If you keep this in mind, you will infuse everything with light.

The days you go through life with a smile as you move through your activities are the moments where we feel your loving energy. It would feel like a light beam bouncing all around the room.

We are here to encourage you to keep your energy full of joy. When you focus on the love, that is when you will do your best work. Go about your life as if miracles will happen around every corner because they will.

Feel great satisfaction in knowing you make a difference just by being you. If you appreciate every moment, you will feel the momentum of energy growing. It is in your loving hands as you prepare a cup of tea and in your embrace when you love another.

Love and light seep through your being when you know you are more than enough. It is our message to your heart. Stay strong and steady so the light can move through you and give you the strength to be you.

We live through your calm energy. It creates a world of refuge for those seeking love in their lives. You are a protective bubble around the planet.

We appreciate everything you do. You are a loving being, and we are excited to see what you are becoming at every moment of your life here on Earth. These times may feel tumultuous to you. Please know it is all for a bigger purpose we are growing into.

Keep your energy high, and you will see the path ahead illuminated.

With great love,
Your Inner Being

Dear Human Being,

There will be days when your energy will feel stuck. It sometimes seems like you need to clear the spaces in your home and heart to gain clarity for the coming days.

Especially when you start a new year, goal, or project. It is time for renewal. The time you spend getting things in order, clearing old things, and ensuring your environment supports you is well spent.

You may think you must keep working and brush the clutter away. Yet, in your mind, it still lingers. Even when we cannot see the physical or mental rubbish that litters our spaces, it puts an obstacle between you and your dreams.

Setting aside a day or two to take care of loose ends will bring you a fresh start.

We are always here to support you on this journey, and if we send constant signals to you about this subject, it is time you take notice. Once you clear away the extra things and worries, you will be free to pursue what you love.

Make a list of the following loose ends you may need to take care of:

-Clearing extra things in rooms, cabinets, closets, or the garage.
-Taking care of recycling or donations set aside.
-Setting up a banking system/financial records.
-Digital tidying on your computer (deleting extra photos or files).
-Clearing out guilt and shame stored in your mind.

Set aside days and times to take care of these things, and your life will open up to many more possibilities.

You will be amazed at how you feel once these items are cleared. It is as if your spirit holds on not only to physical things in your way but spiritual ones. Once you let go and release all of it, you will feel a great weight lifted from your shoulders.

It is with great joy that we share these ideas with you. We know it has been on your mind for a long time. When we choose to release it, new things begin to flow.

Life is like a river. If our thoughts and things impede the flow, our ideas get stuck. To clear the way for your beautiful dreams, you must clean the waters by going through everything. You will notice the difference.

Once you complete those tasks, the world will open up to you!

We are here waiting for you to finish this so we can put more opportunities and signs upon your path. We are so excited for you and all that will transpire in your world today!

Thank you for being a loving part of this universe. We appreciate you with all of our beings.

With great love,
Your Inner Being

Dear Human Being,

We love to see you wake up early to the fresh, clear energy of the morning, ready to do your best work. Those hours provide you the clarity to see part of your path ahead. The mystery of life is always there, but in the newness of the morning light, your ideas will come to life.

It is beautiful to start on your creative endeavors before anyone else arises. All is quiet, and your mind is clear. You can start over every morning, and that is such a gift. The universe grants you a wish in the morning for your dreams to come true.

When you abide by your alarm, the day goes smoothly because you chose yourself. You opted to create a world for yourself and spread your light wherever you go.

As your words flow or your paintbrush hits the paper, you are the creator of worlds. You join you on your quest in the mornings full of promise.

Lighting a candle and sharing what you are grateful for is a beautiful way to wake up your spirit. You can align with all the energy around you, flowing towards your highest good. We jump for joy when we see you start your day with gratitude. It sets the tone for the rest of your waking hours.

Go calmly into your mornings with grace and light. You will feel the difference when you do not rush. Time will work in your favor when you flow seamlessly from task to task. Do not be in a hurry. There is always time to do what is best for you.

As you go about your day, notice your energy levels. When your energy is high, you will constantly feel a smile coming to your face. It is a feeling of deep satisfaction with your life and activities. Hold on to that smile, and know you are going in the right direction. All will be well.

Begin the morning soaring above the clouds in your imagination, and you will go far. When you trust in your dreams, they will appear right in front of your eyes.

We love to see you take steps toward your destiny every day. You do not have to work every single hour to find success in this world. Finding pockets of rest and times to create are the best ways of living in alignment with creation.

We wish you love and light all the days of your life,
Your Inner Being

Dear Human Being,

We know it is challenging to see yourself not holding to the plans you made. You often get upset at yourself or blame yourself when these things happen. Your elaborate, detailed plans can be derailed.

Do not keep yourself in despair and distress. It is natural to have doubts about life and what you can do. From our point of view, every day is beautiful. Yet, the way humans can view it is different. You have a complex life. There is so much to do in one day.

If you feel disappointed about how much you have accomplished, do not worry. Go out to create your life every day. Be easy on your heart. To be here on Earth at this time is a miracle.

Instead of blaming yourself, get curious about your situation. Look upon what you do accomplish with great love and admiration. Applaud yourself for the creativity and caring you send to the world daily. We know you often feel you are not doing enough. Yet, being here to hold the light is more than enough.

Take a look at your situation with a gentle heart and mind. Walk yourself mentally through the day and attach yourself to your feelings. How do you feel when you decide to stop creating for the day? Do you need to rest and allow your body and spirit to recharge?

Examine your life through the lenses of someone who loves you without conditions. There may be a good reason you do not complete your tasks. Consider this before getting angry at yourself.

Take some time to sit quietly by yourself and ponder your choices. What feels right to you? That is the only thing you need to concern yourself with. If it feels right, you will know what actions to take. If it does not, try something else. You are here to experiment with your life and try different paths. Be like a loving scientist with your life and work.

If something is not working for you, you can change it. We are here to support you with loving feelings of joy.

No matter what, we are excited for you to explore your choices. Life is an endless, abundant buffet of colorful fruit. We encourage you to delight yourself with as many as you'd like.

The most beautiful part of life is sorting and choosing. You can go down a path to explore for a while and discern if it is right for you. If not, you can turn around and try another. Being a gentle explorer of life is the way you can free your spirit from worry.

With great love,
Your Inner Being

Dear Human Being,

Sometimes, you will come upon a force in life. It calls on you when you have the best intentions to do things that light you up. Yet, try as you might, you feel defeated.

It is an invisible force, just a faint feeling you encounter from time to time.

Resistance shows up as an uninvited guest in your creative world. When you intend to create, it makes you feel you do not have the will to continue. Or, you may get started and then give up.

This unwelcome intruder in your life is not evil. It is trying to keep you safe and protected. However, to create what you came here to do, you must set boundaries with it. Being firm yet loving with it is the best way.

Let us help you with some words to say to this force when it begins to form a wall between you and your dreams.

Dear Resistance,

We meet again on the edge of my dream world. You show up when I intend to do something out of my comfort zone.

I know you mean well and want to protect me from heartache, doubts, and criticism. However, I need to move forward down this path of discovery on my own. I know there are roadblocks, pitfalls, and deep emotions ahead of me.

Please let me face those on my own. I am not alone because I have my inner being who wants me to shine brighter.

I understand you may think you have my best interests at heart, but not allowing me to have the strength to sit down and do my work is crossing a boundary. Please respect my wishes so I can spread my light through my art.

It may be some time before we meet again, and I wish you all the best, but I know I have the strength to continue my journey.

With love,
A Human Being.

We hope these words help you discover a way forward with the dream you are creating at every moment. We want this for you because it will allow you to become who you are.

We always hold you in a place of discovery, creativity, and fun. Never allow fear to hold you back. Failures are just a way of carving out a path for you to travel.

With great admiration and hope for your present moment, we wish for you to smile upon yourself, for you are radiant with love for everyone.

With great love,
Your Inner Being

Dear Human Being,
Have you ever noticed your dreams floating in whenever you let go and have fun? We love it when that happens! It seems like if you follow your passions, accolades start rolling in.

Do not push for your goals. Gently pull them towards you by loving what you do. That is the magical touch. We jump around with glee and clap our hands. Our cheers for you cannot be heard, but we are the feeling of joy coming over you.

Believing in yourself enough to create your dreams is a big step. You are evolving as a creator. What a wonderful and glorious time to manifest everything close to your heart.

Sometimes, it seems the world around you is in turmoil. If you can stay steady, keep the light in your heart, and hold onto it, your path of discovery will remain open. Do not shut down and give into the darkness. Your light needs to shine bright for others to see the way forward.

When you make something with your whole heart, it is like an electric charge. It sends loving energy to everyone who encounters it and is changed by your words, art, music, dance, or other creative services to the world.

Maintain that energy day by day, and it will grow stronger. When you stay in equilibrium, you have a bright aura that can light up the room. It provides hope for everyone to keep going.

We appreciate you and the work you do every day to keep the Earth evolving. Even when you think your contribution is small, it changes everything.

Thank you for all you do!
With great love,
Your Inner Being

Dear Human Being,

Life can feel scattered, like a trail of crumbs left from eating a doughnut on the sofa. We see you trying to keep order and have a perfect routine. It can be challenging to keep up with your schedule and your dreams.

Please know you are doing your best every day. It may not look like it from your perspective, but from our view, it is perfect. Days flow in the way a river does. Sometimes, there are extra rocks to avoid and other times, it is smooth sailing for your boat of life.

Sometimes, you get a later start, needing to slumber longer. Believe it or not, we are in charge of that. You may blame yourself. Yet, you will feel refreshed and ready to take on challenges.

Everything will happen on its own divine timeline. Do not fear. Your only concern is to shine your light in as many ways as possible daily. The rest will take care of itself.

Turn your worries to the universe, and you will discover what we mean.

Shining your light means doing what you love most and sharing it with others. Some days, you may not feel like you have something to add to the world. Those are the days you may need to create more. Believe us when we say the world needs your exact brand of magic right now.

If you are a writer, share some of your words each day. Likewise, if you sing, dance, paint, cook, or create games, do something to light someone up regularly. The more you hide away, the darker things become for you and everyone around you.

It is like a plant that needs nourishment in the form of sunshine every day, or it will wither and become weak.

Be content by doing just a little bit every day. You do not have to create all your masterpieces in one day. Just work on something small. That is all you need to do. The rest is up to us and the universe. Put your trust and faith in us, and you will thrive.

It brings us great joy when you choose to share your gifts with the world. Please do not hide away and be afraid. Your light is the most precious thing on Earth. When you dim it, you hurt yourself and rob others of the chance of getting to know the true you.

Before you came here, you promised to uphold your light as long as possible. We are here to help you keep that oath. We may send you small glimmers and impulses to do something. It always seems like something intriguing to do. It may confuse you or feel like you are not accomplishing something. Yet, when you follow through on those magical impulses, something will happen.

Success always happens when you are having fun, so go out and celebrate life! There is so much to appreciate and love in this world. Rejoice!

We are here to cheer you on! Keep going!

With love,

Your Inner Being

Dear Human Being,

Some days, you may be confused when you and a loved one disagree. You still love each other. However, you cannot see eye to eye.

Fear not, for you can send your love in many ways.

It is paramount for you not to live in fear. You will diverge from the opinions and truths of those closest to you. It will seem to shatter your world, and you will live in confusion. However, there is a way to live with integrity. We can show you how to go on with your life with love.

Speak your truth to them clearly. Let them know you love them with all your heart, but you may see things from a different perspective from them, and it is perfectly okay. Feel safe and confident in sharing your views. You will not hurt them with your honesty. You must be true to yourself.

It is time to heal. Let it all go. It does not mean you have to agree. Yet, you can live in harmony with your differences.

Send them love through whatever means you deem comfortable. You can send love in prayer, light a candle, setting intentions. Do whatever feels best to you. Listen to your heart and us, your inner being, to guide you. You can do this!

It is best for your heart if you let it all out for the healing to begin. The more you hold your truth inside, the worse it will feel. Communicate in the best way you can, and let it go.

You will feel lighter and more able to move on with your creative life.

We love you with all our being,
Your Inner Being

Dear Human Being,

On dark days in winter, you may feel your light wavering. It sometimes feels like someone took all your energy and ran away. Do not fear. You will get your power back in the coming days.

If your energy feels low, focus on us. We are here to embrace you in our loving light, no matter what your emotions tell you. Our love is steady, calm, and ever-present. It can lift you up on the blackest of nights and propel you forward to great heights.

Add breathing room to your days, especially when you feel low. It means you need to rest and focus on yourself a little more to cause the spark to ignite within your heart once again. All human beings need time to replenish their energy from time to time. It is the best thing you can do for yourself.

If you have little creative energy, try to create something early in the morning. Then, as the day continues, your momentum will still be there. You can rest and take breaks, focusing on positive, uplifting thoughts.

Then, plan a day just for you. One in which you can do something special for yourself and feel renewed once again. Sit in the candlelight as you sip tea and soak your feet in warm, soapy water. Immerse yourself in a floral-scented bath. Do something for your inner and outer spirit to bring back your loving energy.

The love you feel for your work will return to you soon after you take moments to care for your loving heart. This we promise you!

On days when your energy is low, it may seem like you will never be flying high again. Yet, there is always more energy in the world for you. You need to take care of yourself. You are holding the light for others, so you must replenish yourself more often.

Time taken out for yourself is not a waste of time. In fact, it is essential not only to your well-being but that of the planet. When everyone learns to value themselves, their light shines bright!

With great love,

Your Inner Being

Dear Human Being,

We understand you are working hard towards your dreams. Those aspirations will come to fruition at the right time. The most important thing for you to do is do your best work. When you do that, everything else is taken care of.

Focus is the key to everything. It is as if when you are focused on accomplishing your goals, everything else falls by the wayside. It all dissolves into nothingness because you are determined to reach your destination in life.

We urge you to find the time you are most creative and have little resistance. It most often is first thing in the morning. While the rest of the world sleeps, you can create. Many forces may try to stop you, but we hold you in our utmost admiration so that you can complete your tasks.

If resistance calls and tells you to do other things or change your plans, we hold you accountable to your dreams. Our whispers are like a fire burning through you to create something magnificent. It will be the most beautiful creation you have laid eyes on.

Make your steps small, and you will complete your journey faster. It may seem very strange to say something like this. However, big goals come about through daily action.

Our advice to you:

1. Choose only three creative things to focus on per work period.
2. Break them up into small chunks (500 words, 1 design, 1 song)
3. Block out hours to do these and repeat daily.

It is also paramount for you to rest at least one day a week. A creative battery must charge to its full potential to have the energy to bring your dreams into reality.

Once you set this plan into motion, you will see results happen. Right inside your heart, we hold the energy and light every day. Your focus and attention are the greatest gifts.

Do not allow yourself to get distracted and fall off your mission's path. Once creative work is done for the day, there is time to rest, relax, and reflect upon life. We offer this easy plan because we know you will take it and create your best life.

We offer all our love, devotion, and guidance daily. Beating within each heart of humanity lies all the answers each needs to thrive. Paying attention to the signs and signals within life will ensure all will be well.

When you stay on the path and do not succumb to resistance's grasp, feelings of love wash over everything. It is as if magic sprinkles glitter over every surface, lining the skies with hope. It is what dreams are made of, and it is a great honor to come upon them.

Spreading light upon the Earth will heal it. All must come together to create their joy, and it will manifest the frequency needed to make light energy. Each time you enjoy your work, it ripples out as waves of love to everyone.

What you do today may seem small, but it is not insignificant. Choosing to keep walking the path is the best choice every day. We hold you in the highest esteem here within your heart.

Please call on us for any help you may need,

With great love,

Your Inner Being

Dear Human Being,

We know you sometimes ponder life and all its twists and turns. It seems as if there is never a perfect routine, formula, or plan for it. Planning is good, but there are moments in which those fall apart. You can be left wondering how to move forward.

Some days, you may feel on top of the world, like everything is falling into place. Then, a low moment may come upon the horizon, or you procrastinate instead of doing a project. We always hold you in high esteem, no matter what you choose.

As your inner being, we support you with open arms.

Procrastination may always seem like the worst thing in the world to you. Yet, it can be a beautiful pause in life to ponder. Instead of punishing yourself with guilt and shame, get curious about why you are avoiding something.

It can become a loving opportunity to step back and evaluate your priorities. Take some time to be quiet, and go within to listen. Ask yourself the following five questions about your activities:

1. Does it make my heart soar when I think about doing this activity?
2. Does it help others and create a community?
3. How do I feel when I focus on something I love doing?
4. How do I feel when I am doing my favorite activity?
5. Are there some activities I can delegate or stop doing to make time for my passion?

These questions will help you find your true calling and priorities in life. Sometimes, you assign yourself too many things to do and do not have the energy to do what you love. Step back and see what works best for you.

Everyone is unique and has a different energy set point. Not all human beings are alike. You may need to slow down to find the best way toward your dreams. It will all unfold in due time. Never fear: we have your spirit in our loving hands.

One piece of advice we can give you is to keep things simple. Do not try to do more than three activities a day. Of course, take good care of yourself. There may be some minor chores to do to care for your home. Yet, if you keep your list to three items on your work or creativity list, you will soar.

Reducing your list gives your mind, body, and spirit time to rest in between. It will increase your creativity in the long run. If you try to keep working at all times, there may be a shutdown in your abilities. At those times, your body may become ill. You will be forced to take a break. To avoid this, go slow and steady.

Remember the turtle who won the race. It did not worry about its competitors or try to trick the system; it simply walked steadily toward its goal. It is the same for human beings. Keep stepping toward your goal, and you will arrive. Life is not a race. But a slow progression toward your destiny.

When you realize this, everything will change and fall into place.

With great love,
Your Inner Being

DEAR HUMAN BEING,

We understand some days you are tired. It may seem like there is no energy to continue your daily tasks. Yet, we urge you to do something small to make a ripple in the pond of the universe. When you use your gifts, more energy will come your way.

It is our promise to you- shine bright, and more will be given.

You will feel the world weighing down upon your shoulders. Fear not, for you can lift it off and start anew.

When you complete your small task for the day, rest when you are tired. Your energy may come and go, but your heart stays steady as we wait with you. Feel the beautiful energy of the Earth sustaining you.

Call forth the reserves you hold within to bring your dreams into reality so that you may savor them and bring their light into the world.

Some days feel monotonous, and others are filled with bright, shining promise. Trust your emotions and go with the flow of the day. Give attention to your energy and let it guide you on how much to do.

We hold our energy steady, but circumstances are sometimes out of our control. Sometimes, your rest cycles are thrown off, or unforeseen events are happening to capture your attention.

Focus as much as you can on your creative gifts. They will give you energy where your body cannot. Finding the will to continue when you are tired means it is a light you need to illuminate the world.

It is not the kind of power you hold over others to manipulate them, but a gentle, kind power lighting up the Earth with kindness and grace. Once you set out to use it, you will feel as if your lungs are filled with new, fresh air, ready to run to your next destination!

We admire your tenacity every day!

With great love,

Your Inner Being

Dear Human Being,

You may feel deep pain when others do not believe in your dreams as much as you do. We always hold you in the highest regard and know they will manifest. Others may not comprehend the depth of your true belief.

Do not let their views stop your determination to move forward. It is paramount for you to continue down the path you feel is best suited to you.

In life, sometimes you may feel like the outsider, the different one. Everyone seems to be on a different path as you. Hold steady and shine your light because you inspire others seeking to fill their hearts with joy.

When you feel defeated, put more effort into making headway on your dreams. You can prove to yourself it is of utmost importance. At times, it is the contrast that makes you stronger.

We see you sit down to accomplish something you deem worthy of the world. Never dim your light because it does not suit the traditional path. Every soul has a place in this world, and you came to learn your destiny.

Sometimes, there will be a higher hill to climb than you anticipated. Others will stand in the fog, unable to see. You hold the lantern, and it is inside your heart. Be still, and you will find it. Know that you are the one to do this work.

When there is doubt in the air, shine brighter. You will find it within yourself where we reside. We hold the matches and will never let your candle extinguish. Your spirit is eternal and beautiful. Rise up and inspire others to follow their hearts.

You are much stronger than you know. A deep, bold strength rises from you when you decide to share.

Work with love in your heart and find your way. Sometimes, you may need to take a slight detour to help with worldly things. It is not something you must fear but embrace. Know we are with you at every moment. We hold your heart in a loving embrace. You exude love with everything you do out of the goodness of your heart. Souls like you can sometimes be very sensitive to the words and deeds of others. Let your emotions flow, and know you are always loved.

Sometimes, words come out that can hurt your heart, but they are not meant to damage your spirit. It is because others may not comprehend what you aim to do. Living through your heart is a lonely path at times, but you will find comfort in knowing others are with you, along with us.

Every second, someone wishes on a star for their dream to come true. Their prayers are sent to the winds of change. They swirl about on clouds of sparkling dust to settle into their hearts. Their wishes transmute into love and light, ready to help others.

It is love that changes everything. It is capable of a wave of beauty to strengthen the hearts of everyone who touches it. It is the same power you hold within your spirit. Hold onto it, but also set some free. When you give your gifts and talents, you will be free to delight in all the world offers. Grasp your beliefs and fly into the winds of change like a kite ready to set sail. You always have the power and determination to do all that you desire.

With great love,
Your Inner Being

Dear Human Being,

At times, we will send you on a side mission. It may seem to disrupt what you are doing at the time and send you into chaos. However, that is not our intent.

It means you are meant to discover something within yourself that will help you along your path to fulfillment. It does not mean you have failed; quite the opposite. Simply put, the more experiences you have, the more you will align with your true self.

Sometimes, even though you spend time doing things you love, you may veer off your path into a comfort zone. That is when we decide to shake things up a bit. We know it disrupts the flow, but you will see the miracles that come of it.

When you step out to do something completely different, it will change your view of the world.

If it has been a while since you stretched your wings, the time has come. Let the tears flow and then start to wander towards your destiny. Everything you want is waiting there for you to discover.

Explore other avenues and find work you love. You do not have to abandon your dreams; you can still pursue those.

We are always here to allow you to be yourself and offer ways of expressing your talents to benefit others.

There are so many ways to create joy in this world. People are waiting to meet and embrace you. You are needed here on this Earth to make a difference. Things you feel are small ripples become waves until they overtake everything and become joy.

We always bring you signs, signals, and situations for your greatest joy. It may not always feel that way, but it is intended for you to learn from every experience in life. Sometimes, it may be scary to pursue something completely new. Yet, we cheer you on because we believe in you when nobody else does.

Find love for yourself in everything you do, and you will find us beside you. We love to see you stand in your light and shine as brightly as possible.

Please know you are always loved with pure light.

With great love,

Your Inner Being

Dear Human Being,

You need to recharge your body and spirit.

Know it is paramount to take good care of yourself today and always.

At times, we send you signals it is time to slow down.

When your battery runs low, recharge it with positive thoughts and rest. The time you spend taking good care of yourself will translate into the gifts you have to share with the world. Humans often think they must be busy to create their dreams.

However, know that you are always enough, no matter what. You have immense beauty, creativity, and power inside you that lives on for an eternity. Think of the nature of your love! We want to communicate that everything you do is beautiful.

You are loved every single moment of your life by us and others. We reside deep in your heart, always giving you a pep talk for your day. If we were to speak to you out loud, this is what we would say:

Sweetheart, you are capable of so much more than you know. Never doubt every effort you make is loved by us. We have an eternity to be inside your spirit, and happy you chose us. You have infinite possibilities available to you each day. Use those to uplift yourself and others along the way.

Whenever we witness your actions, we applaud you. Every time you try, whether you fail or not does not matter to us. The only thing that matters is doing your best. We know your heart, spirit, and soul because we were there on the day of your creation.

It was a day of celebration and light. A new soul born to take on a life and learn lessons. What a grand and beautiful gift to be here on Earth, the most challenging school for all souls. You chose to be here because you knew it would benefit others.

Never forget why you are here and your mission to spread love to everyone. At this time, your joy is needed for the Earth to heal and come together in happiness. Your message is pure and timely.

We love you with all of the particles and stars in the universe,

Your Inner Being.

Dear Human Being,

Sometimes life changes can be scary. We know staying in your comfort zone always feels better. Yet, you will experience more beauty and creativity outside that circle.

At times, you may come upon something that tests you. It is our way of changing your direction so that you may discover something important about yourself and the world around you. If you embrace it, the world opens up to you.

When you reject change and stay stagnant, it is like a pond of still water. It will attract pests. Staying the same forever does not help you flourish and flow like a beautiful stream.

We wish you to flourish and grow all the days of your life.

With great love,

Your Inner Being

Dear Human Being,

Do not worry about the future; each step you take today is beautiful. Right now, in front of you, is an ever-changing reality. You are an eternal spirit on a brief stay here on Earth. Make the most of the joy you have today to move forward.

Each assignment your soul takes is a new adventure. As you embark upon your day, think of it like traveling. You are there to meet new people, have new experiences, and grow as a human being. That is the only job you need.

Every moment you embrace your whole self, we are delighted. If we had form, we would jump, shout, and dance around with glee. It gives us great happiness when we decide to try something new.

Take each moment gracefully, and you will see a new world open up right before you. There is no need to worry about the past or future. That is the glorious thing about this reality; it contains so many mysteries.

Actually, not knowing something can be a blessing. Trusting in life to lead you where you need to go is paramount. Have faith everything is working out FOR you. It often may not seem that way, but it is the most beautiful thing about living here on Earth.

Since you do not remember your mission here on Earth, we give you reminders. When a particular mode of being starts to stagnate or not work for you, circumstances will carry you to something else.

What an opportunity you have as a human being! We are excited for you each time you venture out of your comfort zone. Strangely, the more you try to accomplish, the more you will get done.

We thank you for your beautiful service every day.

With great love,

Your Inner Being

Dear Human Being,

Isn't it magical to see all the possibilities in life? Life is always more glorious than we think it to be. There are infinite choices available to you at every moment. The more decisions you make, including being joyful, the more will come into your life.

It is always your choice, even when it does not feel that way. Life has a way of making magic happen when you need it most.

A long-lost dream may resurface again. All the connections and resources you need are there to help you thrive. Never lose sight of any plan you follow. It will keep coming up for you over and over until you can find it.

The universe works in mysterious ways, and that is the most magical thing about it. Keep calling in your intentions because you never know what may happen. Tell it what you want to do and what is best for you. It will come true!

Imagine things and think way outside the circle of normality. That is where your dream lies.

Everything works in divine timing, and you are meant to grow and spread your wings out into the vast world. All possibilities exist at one time. There are choice points in your life, but even if you choose a different path, we will find a way to redirect you toward something you wished for.

Out of the blue, others will point out something you had not considered or thought about for a long time. It may then become a focal point for you. Be patient. Life will work out all the details. Just work on what you have under your control, and do not worry about other things.

People will come into your life to help you become the best version of yourself, and you may spread joy. It is the happiness of the universe that is your birthright.

Let everything fall into place, and watch the magic happen right before your eyes. If you were an over-thinker before, you become calm about everything now. Just trust yourself above all else. You always have the answers at this moment because we are here to support you every step of the way.

Life takes care of you more than you can imagine. It will put people, circumstances, and opportunities in front of you so you can run with them and see your dreams take flight!

With great love,
Your Inner Being

Dear Human Being,

We know you wish to see your dreams come true this instant. It is difficult to wait and see how they unfold. Yet, it is there where the joy lies.

Every day, we witness you striving and working towards your aims. You can get a little distracted, but you make progress. That is a win in our books. It is not always easy to believe in yourself at every moment. You may have doubts or not have people who believe in you as we do.

When you feel like everyone is not in your favor, lean on us. We know we are only an inkling, a feeling in your heart, but we are here.

Trust in us and your deepest feelings. Those will allow you to move toward all your wishes, hopes, and dreams.

Sometimes, there is a dream that sleeps deep inside your spirit. You may not know you want it to come out and play, but you do. You may tell yourself to stop thinking about it, but it pops up as you go about your day. Is it meant to be? Watch for the signs all around you.

You will notice people beginning to tell you what your destiny is when you haven't heard it for a long time. Dreams long tucked away may begin to resurface again. It is never too late to have those thoughts that come and go.

Let your destiny unfold one day and one action at a time. Do not rush it or wonder how it will come about. Slowly breathe your way into each moment with glee and purpose. Everything and everyone you need will appear at the right time. Follow your intuition and do what seems right at the time.

You will hear whispers of advice from long ago. Those were our voices, amplified by a human being so you could listen to us. Sometimes, our own ideas brought to us by feelings are not enough. We make sure you get the message.

We love to send you pondering thoughts, full of love and anticipation for what will happen next. It is our great joy to be with you while witnessing your best moments.

All you need to do is follow the next step. We know all humans like to try to skip ahead and guess all the steps for a dream to unfold. However, it is best to take it one day at a time. Your path will be illuminated with love when the time is right.

There are resources to help you with every detail you have ever imagined. It will often feel like everything is in slow motion and you are inside a dream.

You may say to yourself: "Do I dare to dream? Is this happening to me?" Yes, it is! We see the effort you put into all you do and how much you love others. You always deserve the best, and it will all unfold.

Those little rumblings and butterflies in your stomach tell you all you need to know. You are on the verge of something great and magical. We are there to hold you in our highest regard and send you signals to pay attention to how you feel. The joy that bubbles up within you is the best feeling of all!

With great love,
Your Inner Being

Dear Human Being,

When a change is about to happen, it is natural to feel a little stress. That feeling is a growing pain and signals you are soaring toward your dreams.

We know when you get a little off-kilter and want to find the path again. It can feel jarring and uneasy. Not to worry; we are here to bolster your spirit with comfort and love. We are always with you at every moment.

You are never alone.

It may feel as though nobody in this universe understands your exact situation, but we do. It is the most beautiful part of our existence, seeing you grow, change, and evolve ever so slightly every day.

We congratulate you on your progress so far. You are a magical human being, even on your darkest days. Never doubt you are always moving forward and making progress.

With everlasting love,

Your Inner Being.

LETTERS FROM YOUR INNER BEING

Dear Human Being,

Letting go of guilt is a beautiful practice. Sometimes, it can stick to you and be difficult to shake. Yet, when you do, it feels like you can fly free.

You are meant to live in absolute freedom, able to choose whatever path you wish to embark upon.

As a human being, sometimes you limit yourself due to guilt and shame. The "what-ifs" of life often hold you back and keep you thinking small. You can soar beyond all of this and more. Do not allow your mind to tell you there are no other choices.

We are here to let you know we love you no matter what. Even if you cannot tell yourself that, we can.

We care for you as if you were the most precious treasure because you are. No two souls are created equally, and each one decided on a mission to here on Earth. The circumstances you are given are perfect for you.

We know they do not always feel that way, but beautiful lessons await.

Thank you for entrusting your life and destiny to us. We promise to uphold your dreams for you every moment of your life and beyond.

You chose Earth, the most challenging school in the universe, for a reason. Here, there are challenges, problems, heartaches, and more. It is here where you will learn how to love.

Immense, unconditional love is not easy to find, yet you have it inside your heart, and we carry it for you like a precious package. Some days, it feels as if it were about to shatter. Do not worry; we have it here, safe and sound.

We admire you for being so brave and wise on this challenging planet. You are our greatest hope.

With great love,
Your Inner Being.

Dear Human Being,

There will be days when you doubt your dreams and do not know what direction you are going. Never fear! Take your life one step at a time. We are here to guide and hold you in the light during your journey here.

We give you one piece of the puzzle each day and moment so that you can feel confident walking your path.

It is frustrating not knowing where something will lead you. There are always lessons to be learned along the way. You may need to be somewhere to learn something, then you can move on to another adventure.

Life is so complex and beautiful all at the same time. We can see far out ahead all of the sparkling images of the life to come for you. Yet, receiving it all at once would be too much to handle.

That is why our signs are so very subtle. We want to make sure you are ready for what is coming around the corner for you. We promise it is bright, shining, and loving, waiting for you to take hold of these dreams.

What beauty and light you have ahead of you on the path!

Your spirit can imagine all the greatness waiting for you, yet your brain may want to keep you safe. It may give you excuses as to why you cannot step forward on your journey. We know what you are capable of, and it is immense. Do not let anything stop you!

You can picture a beautiful image in your mind's eye of what you want to happen, and it is already there. You are always in the process of creating something for the good of everyone. Focusing on benefiting all involved is the best way forward.

Never fear the future; live in the moment as it is all there is. Take in your surroundings and be infinitely grateful for them. They hold the key to who you are and who you are becoming. Gratitude for everything is what will unlock your ideas to create something magnificent.

We have absolutely no doubts as to what you can accomplish. You are a brilliant light worker, here to hold the world in your heart. You are entrusted to do this work with love, grace, and kindness. The more you can love yourself, the more you will discover.

It is always within your grasp to begin the next step. You do not need to know all the details. Everyone is there to cooperate with your vision; you need to meet them. Take every opportunity to help others with their dreams. It will lead you down the path to yours.

We love you with eternal light,

Your Inner Being.

Dear Human Being,

You are brave for coming here to experience all Earth has to offer. There are many ups and downs, and it may seem impossible to move forward.

If you trust in us, you will go far.

The most important thing we can tell you is this: Do not try to plan or figure out everything in advance. Take small steps towards your dreams every day, then listen. Wait and watch. Magic will begin to open right before your eyes.

If you plan too much, miracles do not have room to spring up in your life. It is always when you least expect it. Dreams will pop up like beautiful flowers all around you.

Take time to explore this world around you, and do not fear anything. You are held in safety. It is challenging to believe sometimes, but you are an eternal being. For this reason, you have all the time in the world to explore the options.

You may come to Earth again to learn more lessons or choose another home. However, you will be able to see all the possibilities forever.

That is the beauty of being a soul. You sign on to learn lessons and understand life and its complexities, and along the way, you create a love for all to experience. What a beautiful life!

We give you little things to experience as well as bigger adventures. You will be given only as much as you can handle. Everything is happening for you, especially when it seems like a disaster. Every impulse you receive to take some action is magical.

Even things like cleaning, rearranging, or other tasks bring discoveries to move you further down your path in life. You never know what you will find or what will spark your interest along the way. Follow the clues in life, and never worry about trying something new.

If you feel like doing something, go for it! We promise you it will lead you towards more breadcrumbs on your trail. Each is like a magic seed, waiting to grow into something for you and humanity.

Keep dreaming, envisioning, and hoping for all you want. Never stop yourself from your greatest desires! It is all within your reach. Often, you do not know that all the people, resources, and plans are already out there waiting for you. Keep imagining it as it takes shape each time you do.

Put your desires out there to the universe and call them in with your heart. It is powerful, strong, and willing to help you create what you want.

Your dreams are there to create as they will lead to a beautiful vision for humanity.

We wish you great love on your journey,

Your Inner Being.

Dear Human Being,

Today is a day for yourself. It is Valentine's Day, and you can decide what it means. The real meaning is not in the physical items you may receive but in the loving way you treat yourself and others.

It is a time to reflect on what makes you unique and who you are. At the core of your heart, you are made of vibrant energy. It never leaves you.

You can tap into the infinite love deep within your spirit. You will find a connection.

Anytime you lose your way, come back to your loving center. It is where we reside, lovingly calling you every day. We communicate with a whisper and ride within the wind. Some moments, you may hear us loud and clear, and other times, our calls are very faint.

We are the voice within you urging you to love yourself above all else. It may seem like a selfish thing to do, but within that radiates love to others. The love you find in your own heart is the most powerful one.

Tapping into your heart center gives your life purpose, color, and sparkle.

You feel like floating on air, streaming with sunshine, and singing with the birds. It is the ultimate sensation of joy rising up within your being. It is what we want for you at every moment of your life.

With Great Love,
Your Inner Being

Dear Human Being,

Never doubt it is okay to take some time to organize yourself before a transition. If you try to squeeze all the regular work you do into your day and work on transitioning, it can lead to fatigue and a sense of feeling loss.

Give yourself the time and space you need to create the life you want.

When you start a new business, job, or hobby, it can take time to adjust. Give yourself a few days of respite, planning, and self-care so that you may thrive in your new life destination.

Do what is needed and let the rest go while preparing for this new adventure. Starting a new career or job can take time to get used to. Allow yourself space to grow. We do not expect seedlings to grow into mature plants overnight. Why expect yourself to have everything under control right away?

It is a slow process unfolding, and we are here to support you. If you feel a nudge to do some activities to prepare yourself, allow time and space.

We encourage you to transition to a new and long-held dream. Go forth and make it happen. We believe every step forward will bring you closer to all you hope for.

You are made of stardust and particles from the universe's best hopes. Use those powers to create something spectacular, and you will see how it will transform over time. We love you at every moment, junction, and fork in your path. It is our wish for you that you find your way to the road of dreams.

Take time to celebrate, take care of yourself, and prepare your home and family for a life of magical proportions. It is all within your power. Your dreams will create a ripple effect for all to enjoy.

With great love,
Your Inner Being

Dear Human Being,

You are making a transition in life, and it is okay to feel anxious about it. Allow yourself time to prepare, to do the things that bring you joy as a part of your celebration onto the next thing for you!

We promise you will find happiness in whatever you are called to do. Each little step is preparation for the next chapter of your life. We give you opportunities in small chunks so that you can handle them one bit at a time.

We will never hand you more than you can take on at one time. You are capable of taking on challenges in your life.

Go with the flow of life, and pieces of your dreams will float by, ready for you to catch them in your basket when you are ready. Think of yourself as a beautiful river being, drifting along in life and capturing what means the most to you.

Your dreams are yours alone, and the right people and circumstances will come along when the time is right. Just because the whole stream has not manifested does not mean it will not come to you.

Grand opportunities are always in the form of little chunks of life.

Like a seed grows and flourishes into a beautiful fruit tree, you will become who you are meant to be. Trust each growth of roots, stems, leaves, and buds, ready to burst onto the scene with perfect timing.

We wish you all the best every single day. You are thriving!

With great love,

Your Inner Being

Dear Human Being,

We understand days where you feel your time is short, yet time is an illusion. All you need to do is follow your intuition; each step of your life becomes magical.

When you feel most overwhelmed, it is the moment to slow down.

It seems counterproductive, but it is the best thing you can do for your spirit. Stop and go outside. Nature is your best teacher. She is always slowly unfolding each petal of her precious flowers right on time. There is no rush.

While life may feel like speeding up or slowing down, it is all in your perception. There is an energy you can tap into even when you feel tired.

As you picked up tiny sticks twirled by the hands of Mother Earth, a calmness rushed to every cell in your body, bringing peace to your soul. Gathering gifts from nature is a beautiful activity, creating new dreams within your heart at every turn.

Whenever you feel disquiet, go outdoors to discover who you are. We promise it is the best solution to all the problems in your life. You will feel instantly refreshed, and worries will seem far away from where they once were.

Take solace in every step on your garden path. It is the road to miracles.

With love,
Your Inner Being

Dear Human Being,

We feel your inner drive to grow with every heartbeat. Your dreams come alive every time you take action.

Some days, you may not feel a burst of energy to complete all your tasks to the best of your ability.

Yet, we want to encourage you to find that extra bit of strength. If you cannot spend as much time as you would like, spend ten or fifteen minutes on your goals.

Each little bit you do brings you closer to what you envision. Where we live within you, there is no time, only a continual present moment. When you decide to do even a tiny amount of a task, a spark ignites within you.

Every inch is part of that mile you are striving for.

Do not give up when you feel down, discouraged, or with low energy. We are here to lift you up if you show some effort. We can already witness those events that seem far away from you. They are happening right now in our eyes!

Time is only a construct to help you structure your days. Seemingly magical things will happen when you give some extra energy to what you desire for yourself. It is not selfish to put in the work.

Your wildest dreams await you on the other side of those fifteen minutes!

With our greatest love,
Your Inner Being

Dear Human Being,

We want to let you in on a little secret. The more you move your body and become active, the more ideas you will have that will lead to creating your dreams.

It is as if every cell in your body switches on with loving momentum.

Do you ever wonder why you get more ideas the more you work out, walk, or run? Ideas flow more, just like a river free from stagnation.

If you sit too much each day, ideas sit with you. However, if you make time each day to do some exercise, your mind shakes up new ways to meet your destiny!

How amazing is that?

It is why many creative people go for walks in nature or on a trail to get new ideas.

Find more ways to activate yourself, and you will see a difference in your life. We nudge you towards more things that will help you the more you activate your heart. When your body flows, we are ecstatic!

You will see more progress in your life, guaranteed!

With a love for an active lifestyle,

Your Inner Being

Dear Human Being,

Whenever overwhelm hits you, take a moment to pause. Having a to-do list can be a gift in disguise. It means you have a beautiful life to live.

Every evening, make a list of tasks for the next day. We love to experience those lists because it means a plan is forming. It does not mean you must complete everything on it, however.

The next day, evaluate your list and take a moment to feel what your heart knows about it.

It may seem strange to ask your heart about a list, but it knows what activities will lead you to your dreams and which can wait.

Even if the list is long, pare it down to three goals for the day. Save your longer list. If you have time, you may choose to do some of those other activities. If not, allow yourself to celebrate your accomplishments and move on to the next day.

We love to see you crush your goals!

With great love,

Your Inner Being

Dear Human Being,

Do you know the feeling when something on your dream list actually happens? If you could see our inner smile, you'd smile too!

There is a magical formula we'd love to share with you.

Write down your dreams constantly. Look at them as many times a day as possible. Cut out photos of things and experiences. Do not limit what you write down.

If something changes, change your list. Every time someone mentions an experience such as travel, and you want to go, add it to your list. Nothing is off-limits here. It is your space! Writing with a pen and paper is a beautiful experience. It can bring sunshine into your life in an instant.

The best thing you can do is have fun with it. If you want to rewrite it later, that is perfect!

You can keep your dream book and pull it out multiple times daily.

We are squealing with excitement here!

With great love,

Your Inner Being

Dear Human Being,

Maintaining your commitment to a goal can be challenging at times.

Allow yourself grace when going for your dreams.

For example, if you set a goal to become a runner, start with a gentle pace and a few minutes daily. Gradually add more as you become stronger. If there is a day when you are short on time, run only five or ten minutes.

Keep your hopes alive- like a little candle flickering, you will succeed.

Momentum for humans is the secret to achieving in life. Decide to take a small action daily. You will surely reap the benefits over time. Life loves it when you go for it!

With great love,
Your Inner Being

Dear Human Being,

It can be painful to watch someone going through a tough time. You want to help but are unsure what to do. We know it hurts your heart.

While we reside in every human's spirit, your loved one may not be able to hear our whispers when their physical or mental pain is severe. They are often unable to engage as much with life as they once did because outside circumstances cause them to be in a dark space.

You will want to shine bright for them.

However, they sometimes cannot access that light for a while. We encourage you to take good care of yourself during this time. Your outpouring of energy towards them is intensely loving, but it can take a toll on you.

Send them good energy, comforting prayers, and love. They will find the bright spots in life over time. We promise you this!

They are loved and supported beyond their wildest dreams.

Offer messages of support, good humor, and beauty. Loving someone is the best way through, always! We hold them in our loving space. Trust that life will help them in the best way possible to find joy and their path forward.

With great love,
Your Inner Being

Dear Human Being,

When you first start a new habit, it may seem daunting. The first minute you attempt running again may feel agonizing. Your body is getting used to what your soul wants you to do.

However, when you make a daily promise, miracles will happen.

The easier way in life is to make excuses like the following:

I cannot run because....it's raining today, I'm short on time, I am tired, I don't have the energy, It won't matter if I skip a day.

All these are your mind (not us) trying to keep you in your comfort zone. It is the zone where everything feels pleasant, but it is not the training ground for growth. Everything outside the circle where you feel safe is where you are meant to travel.

When you keep a promise to yourself, you honor a special bond with your true self. This is who wants you to succeed and go far in life.

We are always on your side and whisper gently in your ear to get going, even if you do not feel like it, because we know you will love the results when you stick with something! The little whisper that says: "Go for it!" is us!

We wish you progress with our greatest love,
Trista

Dear Human Being,

When you feel that inner drive to go for your dreams, our spirit reaches out to your heart. We connect with you daily, hoping you will be able to receive our guidance.

Every time you take an action, we send you a spiritual high-five for your efforts!

We are everywhere and nowhere at the same time. It feels mysterious, but we assure you we are on your side. Just like an executive may have a personal assistant to help with tasks and encourage them to move forward, we fill that role in your life.

Those gentle nudges you feel as you move closer to your destiny are your inner being team pulling you with invisible, loving energy.

Even when you feel alone, you are not. You have a whole energetic team behind you!

Thank you for doing your part to help move humanity forward. Your loving thoughts, actions, and presence are just what we need to go toward a beautiful life. Thank you for being as you are. Just existing here and following your trail of joy, you matter!

With great love,
Your Inner Being

Dear Human Being,

Don't forget to include some wandering time in your days. We often leave delightful little clues we hope you will stumble upon.

A colorful flower, a fallen leaf, the freshness of a raindrop on a blossom. All of these can help you smile even on a dark day. Our wish for you is that in your random walks, you may discover something new about yourself.

We love to leave you signs to delight and surprise you!

Even five minutes a day of aimless steps may help you reach heights you never knew you could. We introduce as much beauty as possible into your days.

You deserve all the best!

With great love,

Your Inner Being

Dear Human Being,

When a loved one leaves this Earth and returns to the spirit realm, it can leave you with feelings of deep sadness and grief. Be with those feelings and allow yourself to let out your emotions.

It is paramount to feel those waves of sadness wash over you. They will heal you in time.

There is no rush to return to normal, as it takes time to heal when the wound of a dear one leaving comes into your experience.

We are here to comfort you during your time of mourning and sorrow.

This life is beautiful, but it is also short. We must know that our loved ones feel joy in the spirit realm, and they may leave loving signs for us to discover. They still watch over us during our daily lives.

We gently hold your hand and guide you through this dark time, knowing the light will enter your heart once again very soon.

Be well and know all is taken care of.

We love you so much!

With great love,

Your Inner Being

Dear Human Being,

Spending time with people who fill your heart with joy allows you to generate more energy to do what you love. We love it when you enjoy life, ponder, wander, and do what makes you happy.

It is in these moments that you shine with infinite possibilities!

Although it is fantastic to be productive, you will find the days you relax are also valuable to your soul's work here on Earth. When you sink into comfort and meditate on the peaceful moments, you will find sparks of joy waiting for you.

Let your heart be open as you tiptoe through the day. Surprises and miracles are right around the corner.

With great love,
Your Inner Being

Dear Human Being,
Do not hold yourself back from trying new things.

It can be as simple as ordering something other than your usual at the coffee shop or challenging yourself to run five more minutes than you did yesterday. You expand your mind, heart, and soul all at the same time.

Stretching your inner and outer limits creates a new life for you, one bit at a time.

We are ecstatic when you push your boundaries! Keep on striving for what you desire in life. There is no goal too big for you to achieve if you put your mind to it!!

Our hearts light up for you!!
With great love,
Your Inner Being

Dear Human Being,

The more you motivate yourself to complete your projects, the more miracles will come to you. Life and the universe love it when you are on fire with creativity!

Positive energy swirls around you as you stick to your schedule, complete your tasks, and remain focused on your dreams. It is all possible and so much more. We feel a tingle of excitement as you step toward your goals daily.

The path rises up to meet you when you say yes to life.

We are here to guide you and support you on your way. Acting as your ever-present friend, we salute each effort you make. Even when you stumble on the road, we pick you up and encourage you to keep walking.

Each time you choose yourself, more loving energy is added to your being. Challenges are there to keep you strong, sharp, and willing to put in the work to get where you want to go.

You are here to do something nobody else can do. Keep showing up!

With great love,
Your Inner Being

Dear Human Being,

Sometimes, you must take action if there is too much darkness in your life. Just like a bush or a tree with too many branches blocking the sunshine, you may need to prune some things in your life. Let in the light!

A plant will grow, thrive, and bloom more when more bright rays reach it. The same is true for human beings.

Cut away any thoughts or activities that darken your path to greatness. You are the leader with the pruning shears! Trim back feelings of not being enough, doubts about yourself, or nagging thoughts no longer serving you.

Take charge by getting rid of anything darkening your way forward!

We are sure of your greatness every moment of your life and hold the light for you. Never doubt you can do it! Take opportunities headed your way and trim back dead branches blocking you. You are meant for more greatness than you ever imagined.

Be the gardener in your life and let in the light!

With great love,

Your Inner Being

Dear Human Being,

Sometimes, an illness or allergy may zap you of your exuberant energy. It can be frustrating to live through those days. We know you always want to participate in lots of activities.

However, it can be an opportunity in disguise.

Take this time to rest, hydrate, and go within your heart. Your body is speaking to you. What is it saying?

Perhaps it is a time to clear away old thoughts irritating you and your progress toward goals. You can also use it to remain more in the present moment. Look around you and feel grateful for all the beauty in your life.

Whenever there is something unwanted in life, it can be used for something positive. You may not have the energy to do your usual activities. However, you can participate in small ways by noticing how you feel, what lights you up, and what helps you feel better.

It is more than okay to not be doing things all the time. Now is the moment for you to know you are perfect as you are. You do not have to do anything to be loved or accepted.

We love you so much! Wishing you perfect health and joy!

With great love,

Your Inner Being

Dear Human Being,

Events can sometimes feel like accidents or not meant to be. They can feel catastrophic and can turn your days upside down.

However, we promise you one thing: they are here to help you achieve your mission in life.

Without these powerful experiences, humans cannot grow to their full potential. If everything is running perfectly all the time, there is no room to expand or dream of other possibilities. At the moment, it is more than okay to grieve. You want your life to return to normal, and it feels scary.

Yet, what is next will bring you joy if you can learn the lessons. Everything in life that seems terrible from the outside is perfect on the inside.

We never want to see you suffer, but you know you are expanding in beautiful ways at the same time. Hidden miracles abound if you choose to be aware of them.

Let us guide you to take steps, even out of the most challenging circumstances.

With great love,
Your Inner Being

Dear Human Being,

When a friend or loved one is suffering, it may be challenging for you to know how to help them. Their pain may be physical, emotional, or psychological. You have a loving heart and will understand how to assist them if you go within.

Breathe to get still and feel what they are going through.

When the ones we love are in crisis, it can bring heartache. We want to take away their pain. It is natural for humans to feel a deep empathy toward others going through a challenging time in life.

It is okay to ask them how best to help. Sometimes, being there with them is helpful. An act of service or a care package will lift their spirits. There is a balance between trying to help too much and being a supportive friend.

Check with them when you can, and offer to listen. Often, allowing them to open up about their pain will be beneficial. We all want a listening ear in our lives.

One of the most important things to do is to not judge their pain. We do not know their life's path, and we each have a unique journey. What is best at this time is to remain open, compassionate, and loving.

Keep your heart open to let love flow!

With great love,

Your Inner Being

Dear Human Being,

When you are working hard toward your goals, it is okay to reevaluate them from time to time. They may need reworking, or you may want to let one go for a while.

While action can help your dreams come true, humans often spread themselves too thin. Take a moment to go over your goals.

Here is a list of things to consider:

1. Does this goal still light your heart on fire?
2. Do you have a list of more than 3 goals?
3. Do you have strategies and daily habits set up for these goals?
4. Are there dates on your calendar for actions related to these goals?
5. Do you have time set aside to achieve these goals?

These questions can help you decide to go toward a goal. Sometimes, if a goal is no longer lighting your heart on fire, it is okay to let it go or at least table it for a while.

Also, we advise you to focus on a maximum of three goals at a time. This way, you will have enough time to accomplish them. If there are extra goals, you may wish to save them after you reach your other goals.

Write your goals down in a notebook you love. Feel free to rewrite them often when you have new details or ideas about them. Reviewing them at least once, two or three times daily- is ideal!

We wish you the best in achieving your aims! You've got this!

With great love,
Your Inner Being

Dear Human Being,

Today, you may feel progress toward your dreams is moving very slowly. Yet, we see your spark, drive, and determination daily!

We understand how much you want to reach your destination. The slow, progressive walk to your destiny is a dazzling journey. Applaud yourself for each small task accomplished, and give yourself grace for days when you do not get as much done.

Everything will happen for you in due time!

We will keep this message short so you can tackle a small item on your to-do list! You can do anything you set your heart and mind to!

With our greatest love,

Your Inner Being

Dear Human Being,

When you chose to come to Earth, it was not a light decision. It is the most challenging place to be, learn, and grow as a human and soul.

For this reason, we always say you are strong and brave.

You have so much more power than you can imagine, being a part of the human family. You all are a tribe coming from one source.

Whatever your challenges, you can get through them. We applaud every effort and understand when you feel frustrated or angry when things are difficult. Be with those emotions and honor them. You are enough at every moment.

Stay and feel everything you need to in that instant.

Sometimes, you cannot see the light when all is dark around you. You search and see nothing but blackness. Yet, we are always here shining.

Once the challenges subside and you come to a place of peace, you might hear our voice in the distance, whispering to get up and join life again.

Your mission is paramount in this lifetime. Nobody else can do what you came here to complete. It is why our message to you is an urgent matter. When you can endure the rough patches in life, your strength afterward will be unstoppable.

Thank you for being here through it all.

With our greatest love,

Your Inner Being

Dear Human Being,

It is natural to judge others based on your unique life's viewpoint. Judging is a way of staying safe in a lot of instances. However, do not let your judgments cloud your relationships.

You may think you know about someone's life and their challenges. Yet, often, you only know what they may tell you. Use all of your senses to stay present and get to know a person before you allow your opinions of their situation to enter your thoughts or conversation.

Stay open and let your heart guide you.

If you can sit quietly and listen, you will find the truth. It will change how you view others and give you new perspectives on their lives.

Realize what they are living through is something you may experience one day. Keep the doors to your mind wide open and discover the lessons hidden behind them. Today, you may feel on top of the world, but if someone is suffering, give them compassion and love.

Everyone goes through setbacks, heartache, pain, and challenges in their lifetime. The support you offer to someone else will come to you in a time of need. Be loving, giving, and free to express your heart's call to action.

With great love,
Your Inner Being

Dear Human Being,

Sometimes, you may want to give up on a project or an idea that does not bear fruit. We know it is natural to feel defeated if your results are lackluster. You may think your failures mean you should stop. However, we want to encourage you to keep going.

If you feel like quitting, stop for a while.

Allow yourself to fully feel your emotions and investigate as if you were a scientist in your own life. Take a walk in nature, and give it time to process.

After a while, you may notice renewed energy beginning to well up inside you. New ideas may pop up in your mind out of nowhere. Wink! That is us trying to get your attention. Commit to your idea a while longer to see where it will go.

Success is an ongoing project. It takes time, dedication, and daily habits to move forward. We have some ideas to share with you on this subject.

1. Commit to your idea for a certain period. The minimum should be six months, and the maximum a year to eighteen months.
2. Your mind may try to convince you to quit sooner. Do not let it!
3. Write down how you will incorporate this project into your daily or weekly schedule.
4. Do not beat yourself up if you have a setback or take some time away. Recommit yourself and begin again with no judgments.
5. Act on those impulses and ideas you receive around your project.
6. Be kind to yourself!

We send you love and know you will accomplish great things! With great love,

Your Inner Being

Dear Human Being,

Despite whatever technology comes into being, your creativity is your greatest strength. Use it every day to thrive!

The ideas you work with are unique and beautiful! There will never be the same combination of who you are. You are tasked with carrying out a fantastic mission during your lifetime, and only you can complete it.

Exercise your ability to come up with ideas every day. Whatever problems come into your life are there for you to creatively solve them. Through these experiences, you gain enormous strength and courage to face challenges.

With enormous love and gratitude for your creativity,
Your Inner Being

Dear Human Being,

Your imagination is your greatest ally. When you trust in your wildest dreams, life will reward you.

Our sincere hope resides in your heart.

More than a body experiencing everything on the Earth plane. You are a spiritual being. Your spirit is resilient, magnificent, and ready to take action on your mission.

Whatever you choose to do, you will learn something from the experience. Every day is a training ground, and it will surprise and delight you.

Our message today is short and sweet- enjoy life!

With our greatest love,

Your Inner Being

Dear Human Being,

Our final letter to you makes us smile with great hope. We know these times are challenging, but you came here to rise to the occasion. You are here at a unique time in history, no matter when you read this. It is your time to shine bright!

Use your insights, feelings, and heart to navigate life. We are always here to support you. You are never alone.

Carry our message forward with you inside your heart. Stay strong and on the light side of life. We believe in you and know you will finish your mission here on Earth. You have all the time needed to accomplish your big goals and dreams.

Do not give up!

When you think all is lost, look within. There, you will find us waiting to cheer you on to the finish of life, no matter what you have going on. You can do it!

We are your greatest cheerleader, rooting for you. Reach deep within yourself to find new energy, courage, and fortitude to do what is necessary to lift your dreams up to new levels. You will be surprised at how much you can do when your heart is in alignment.

With our greatest love and encouragement for a fantastic life,
Your Inner Being

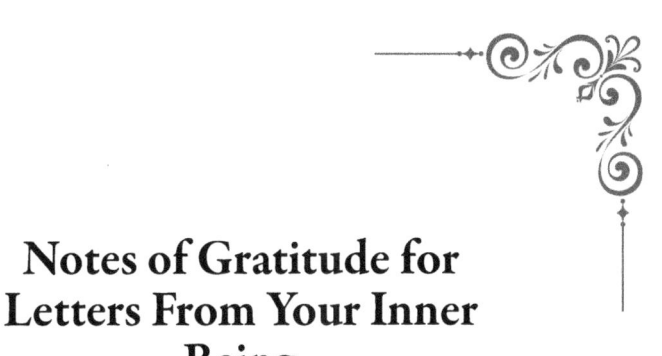

Notes of Gratitude for Letters From Your Inner Being

As humans, we are never alone. Appreciation and gratitude are sources of joy in my life, and I want to thank so many wonderful people who helped birth this book.

First, my loving family at home. My husband Paul is my biggest supporter, always encouraging me in the direction of my dreams. My amazing son Adam is just like his dad, wonderful in every way. He always tells me to go for it!

Loving gratitude to my friend and soul sister, Melissa Bee, for her dedication, friendship, and hard work in writing the foreword to this book. We met while writing on Medium in 2020, and our connection is strong! Thank you, Melissa, for believing in the positive power this book offers for all humankind!

I want to thank my loving parents, Serena and Dale, for teaching me the importance of creativity in life. My dad, a woodworker, and my mom, a weaver, artist, and teacher, taught me to value my creativity.

Thank you to my brother, Stuart, for his great advice about photography, and encouraging me to use my fancy camera and my natural talents for design. I love and appreciate my sister in law Kim for always being so sweet, kind, and loving. Her support means the world to me.

Thank you to my beautiful friends of a lifetime, Lily, Miguel, Lynn, Carol, JoAnn, Fairouz, Melissa, Sarah, Diana, Bev, Michelle, Famke, and Sarah. Your unwavering support of my endeavors fills my heart with joy. I appreciate all of you for being there through everything.

I especially want to thank my best friend and sister, Lily and my dearest friend Miguel. Their support and love shines through the miles that separate us. I met them in Mexico as an exchange student many years ago. Their friendship is always in my heart.

I also deeply appreciate my friends on Medium. Ever since 2020, I have made many international friends through this platform. Thank you for reading my work weekly and for your friendship! I especially want to thank Amy, Pockett, Rebecca, Hollie, Vidya, Lu, Genius, Liberty, Annelise, Gabriella, Dr. Preeti, Gurpreet, and many more for your loving friendship.

About the author

Trista Ainsworth is a writer, pastry chef, video creator, wife, and mother. She loves to find the joy and lessons in her everyday life, and share them through her writing. She writes weekly on Medium in her publication "*Optimism and Light*," and on her Substack newsletter "*Letters From Your Inner Being.*" She also enjoys creating tea-pairing videos on her YouTube channel, Zerocasualteas.

She works three days a week as a pastry chef at Skywater Tea House in Hillsboro, Oregon, and enjoys baking with sourdough at home. Her other loves in life include going on local food adventures with her husband and son, and world travel. Her outlook on life is one of optimism and joy. She wishes for every human being to know they matter and have gifts to share with the world.

About Melissa Bee

Melissa is a loving mom to three wonderful children, a teacher, and a writer. She loves to create amazing memories and experiences with those close to her. She and I met while writing on Medium in 2020. Her poetry and stories took my breath away and we became fast friends. I appreciate her kindness, enthusiasm, and creativity in life.

Don't miss out!

Visit the website below and you can sign up to receive emails whenever Trista Ainsworth publishes a new book. There's no charge and no obligation.

https://books2read.com/r/B-A-XDNU-NJGCC

BOOKS 2 READ

Connecting independent readers to independent writers.

Milton Keynes UK
Ingram Content Group UK Ltd.
UKHW040819141124
451205UK00001B/63